To Aunt Jo
from
Louise

Christmas 1975

The Pleasure of Jewelry and Gemstones

The Pleasure of Jewelry and Gemstones

Joseph Sataloff
and Alison Richards

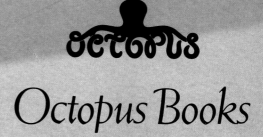

OCTOPUS

Octopus Books

Contents

The Purpose of Jewelry

Man has always worn some form of jewelry, and the need for self adornment would appear to be very deeply rooted. Jewelry has been associated with the four aspects of civilized life with which man has universally been most concerned; money, power, religion and love. It is a little tenuous to stretch this assertion to cover a fifth, war, but it is not insignificant that successful warriors have frequently been rewarded with jeweled decorations, displayed as symbols of their victories.

All over the world, since earliest times jewelry has had religious significance and superstitious associations. The Egyptians believed that their jewelry possessed magical powers; they wore amulets for protection against misfortune and the displeasure of the gods, while even today people wear St Christopher medallions to protect them from disasters when travelling. For many centuries the exclusive patrons of goldsmiths were the wealthy and powerful; today jewelry is still one of the most apparent expressions of status and wealth, because extremely rare and expensive materials have always been employed in its manufacture. Since the introduction of mass production techniques, two hundred years ago, and changes in the social structure, anybody who wishes to wear jewelry, does so. Most women do so for another ancient reason – to make themselves more attractive. Finally, jewelry has always had sentimental and romantic connotations, regardless of its value. Betrothal rings first appeared in Roman times, and have continued for two millenium as a symbol of marriage. The forms of betrothal and wedding rings have often changed over the centuries; the plain gold band now associated with weddings is a relatively new introduction. For many centuries lovers have exchanged lockets containing a portrait or personal momento, such as a lock of hair. The purpose of this book is to outline the development of jewelry, particularly in the western world, from its earliest forms to the work of the present day, which can be seen in shop windows all over the world. The book also sets out to help the collector identify techniques, materials, styles and dates.

First published 1975 by
Octopus Books Limited
59 Grosvenor Street, London W1

ISBN 0 7064 0384 3

Distributed in USA by
Crescent Books
a division of Crown Publishers Inc
419 Park Avenue South
New York, N. Y. 10016

Distributed in Australia by
Rigby Limited
30 North Terrace, Kent Town
Adelaide, South Australia 5067

Produced by Mandarin Publishers Limited
14 Westlands Road, Quarry Bay, Hong Kong

Printed in Hong Kong

Jewelry from Antiquity to the Middle Ages

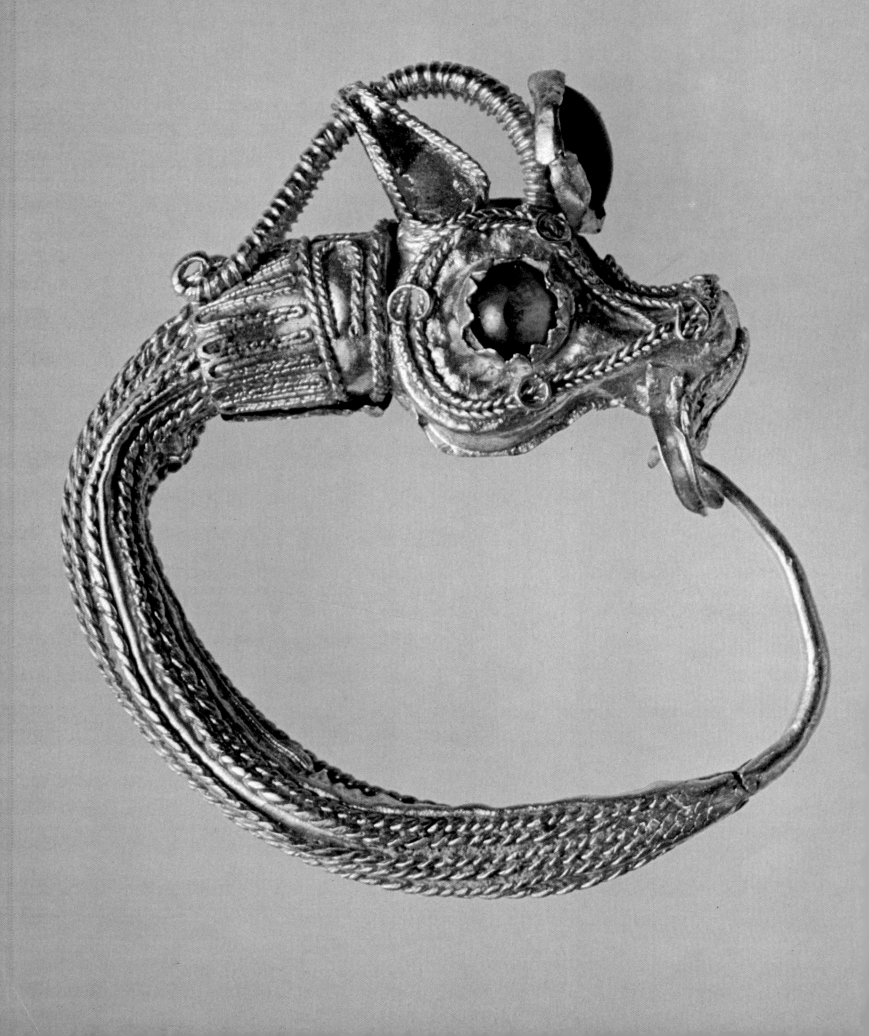

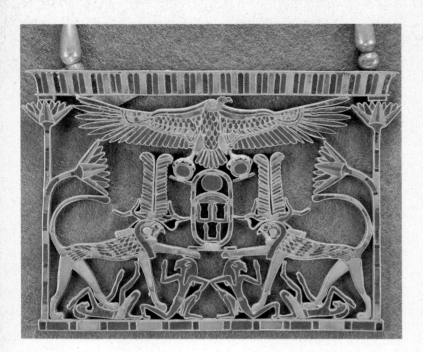

The Egyptians were amongst the earliest producers of fine jewelry using gold and precious stones. Probably all members of Egyptian society wore some form of jewelry, the poorest possessing at least a string of beads or shells; but it was the king and his officials who were the gold-smiths' great patrons. The king made presentations to his courtiers as rewards, whilst in turn they made presentations to their dependants. Bracelets, necklaces, head dresses and huge pectorals were amongst the many forms of jewelry worn by both men and women. The brilliant polychromy of Egyptian work is its outstanding feature, either in complex bead patterns or stone inlay. Cornelian, Turquoise (from Sinai) and Lapis (from Afghanistan) were the favourite stones, symbolizing earth, sky and sea. Gold was lavishly used and was thought to be a form of of the sun solidified; consequently it was highly valued since sunworship was the central feature of Egyptian religion. The inlaid designs were also generally of religious significance and showed deities, many of which had animal forms, for example, the cobra goddess Buto or Nekhebet, the vulture goddess, protectress of Upper Egypt. The main purpose of the jewelry was prophylactic and it was worn to protect the wearer from misfortune and disease. Protection was equally important after death, as has been shown by the wealth of fabulous jewelry found in tombs such as that of Tutankhamun. The finest Egyptian jewelry dates from the twelfth dynasty of the Middle Kingdom circa 2200–2000 BC.

THIS PAGE Egyptian beads and pectoral, see following page. LEFT A gold and garnet earring, Greek, c 300 BC.

PAGE 1 Portrait of Madame de Senonnes by Ingres.
PAGES 2–3 The Hildesheim crown, German, 11th century.
PAGES 4–5 Two French Gothic revival brooches, 19th century.

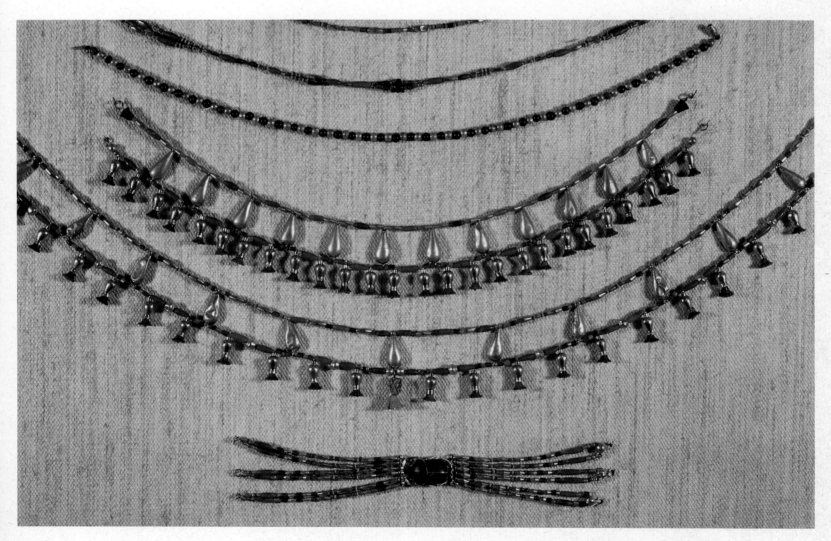

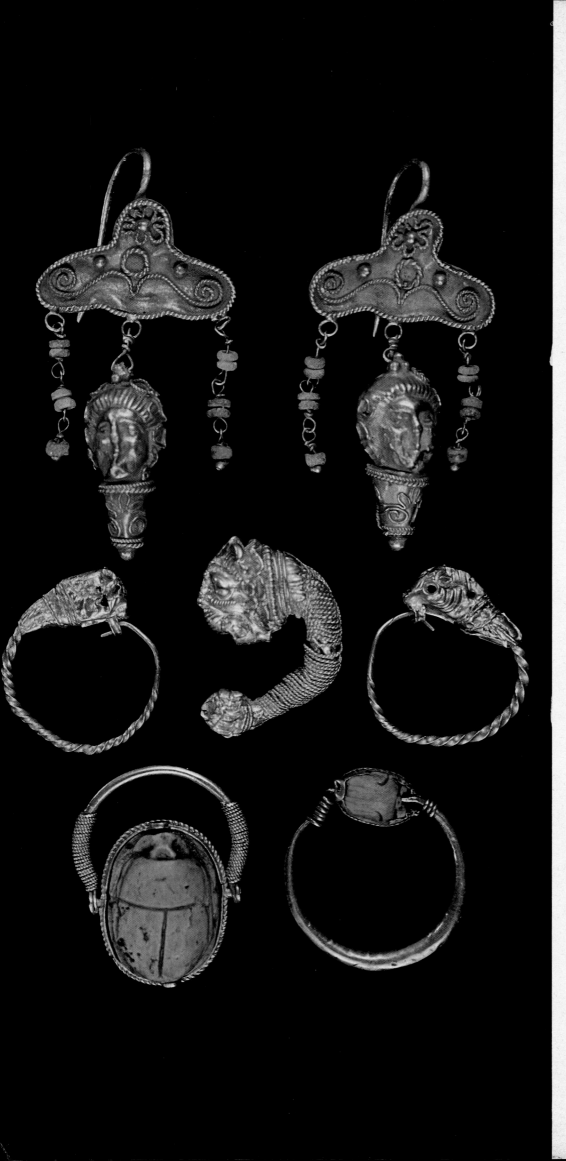

EGYPTIAN JEWELRY

PREVIOUS PAGES ABOVE A gold pectoral inlaid with semi precious stones, including cornelian, turquoise and lapis lazuli. It belonged to King Sesostris III of the twelfth dynasty (Middle Kingdom) and hangs from a necklace made of oblong and round beads of gold and cornelian. This beautifully harmonious design depicts apes with hawks' heads trampling on the vanquished, symbolizing the pharoah's victory over his enemies.

BELOW The Egyptians used thin fine gold combined with brightly coloured stones, fayence and glass, for both bead work and inlay. Fayence is earthenware glazed with crusted quartz mixed with lime, potash and sodium carbonate and then fired. These beads show a variety of sophisticated necklaces dating from the eighteenth dynasty circa 1360 BC, made of gold, lapis, cornelian, turquoise and glass. The centrepiece of the bracelet at the bottom of the picture is a scarab carved in lapis.

GREEK AND ROMAN CLASSICAL JEWELRY

The Greeks did not share the Egyptians' love of colour, instead they concentrated on the delicate detailed decoration of gold with granulation and wire, often twisted, and raised patterns.

LEFT Two types of earrings found all over the Mediterranean. The top pair have female heads made of fine gold hammered into a bronze mould. The gold is high carat and extremely thin. In the middle are a pair of bulls' head earrings and part of a lion's head earring. Sheep and goats' heads were also used for this type, and they were all worn with the head facing the ear.
Below are two Egyptian scarab rings.

RIGHT Two earrings of the more ornate Hellenistic period 330–27 BC. The eye of the gazelle head (left) is set with a garnet; later coloured stones or glass were threaded onto the hoop giving a more colourful effect. On the right a winged diety, possibly Pan, is depicted.

8

From about 1200 BC, the Greek civilization began to influence the whole of the Mediterranean. Besides being gifted architects and sculptors, the people of the Aegean were highly skilled jewelers. The earliest outstanding goldsmiths were in Crete and Mycenae. Later the Etruscans, who settled in Northern Italy in the area now known as Tuscany became the most brilliant jewelers of the classical age.

The jewelry produced around the Mediterranean during the period of Greek dominance 1200 BC to first century BC has many similarities. The main feature is the exclusive use of metal—gold, silver, bronze or electrum. Very little colour in the form of stones was introduced until the Roman era. Instead the craftsmen used skilled decorative techniques such as repoussé, filigree and granulation to embellish the surface of the gold. Repoussé work, a pattern raised in the metal by beating it, was one of the earliest techniques used. Granulation became the speciality of the Etruscans. This process of decorating a solid gold surface with tiny granules of gold was never executed more finely, and the secret of such exquisite work was lost in the Roman period and was not to be

ABOVE Wreaths were an essential part of Greek and Roman dress; they were worn at parties and in processions and were buried with the dead. They were made either of real leaves, or of imitations in gold or silver. This piece is composed of gold ivy leaves. Myrtle leaves were popular, since they were believed to dispel alcohol fumes at parties.

LEFT These three earrings of Etruscan origin circa 700–500 BC show some of the variety and technical brilliance characteristic of their work. The round openwork earring has been pierced out with a chisel and decorated with granulation and repoussé. The two other earrings are of the type generally known as 'baule', probably because they were thought to resemble a valise or bag.

FAR LEFT A fine gold necklace of the early 4th century from Tarentum, now Taranto. Necklaces were not as common as rings or earrings. It is composed of linked rosettes from which hang human heads and buds, illustrating the popularity of naturalism in Greek design. Although this piece appears substantial, it is in fact light, since the heads and buds are hollow.

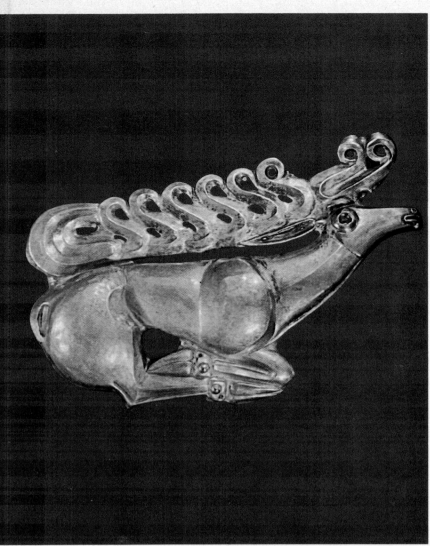

rediscovered until the 1930s.

The conquests of Alexander the Great in the fourth century BC spread as far as north India and Scythia in what is now southern Russia and opened up huge resources of gold for Greece. The reign of Alexander saw the great flowering of Greek art, during which huge quantities of jewelry was made in increasingly elaborate styles.

The Romans continued to follow the Greek patterns, but they used more stones, particularly garnets and emeralds. There was less intricate surface decoration and filigree and granulation became cruder. The chief contribution of the Romans to the jeweler's art was their intaglio work—the engraving or carving of gems. The engraving of hard stones was begun in the fourth century BC by the Greeks, but the Romans developed the skill considerably. They also introduced the method of carving onyx into cameos.

After the fall of the Roman Empire, Europe was dominated for several centuries by successive groups of invaders from eastern Europe and Asia. The Goths and Visigoths, the Franks, the Huns, the Angles and the

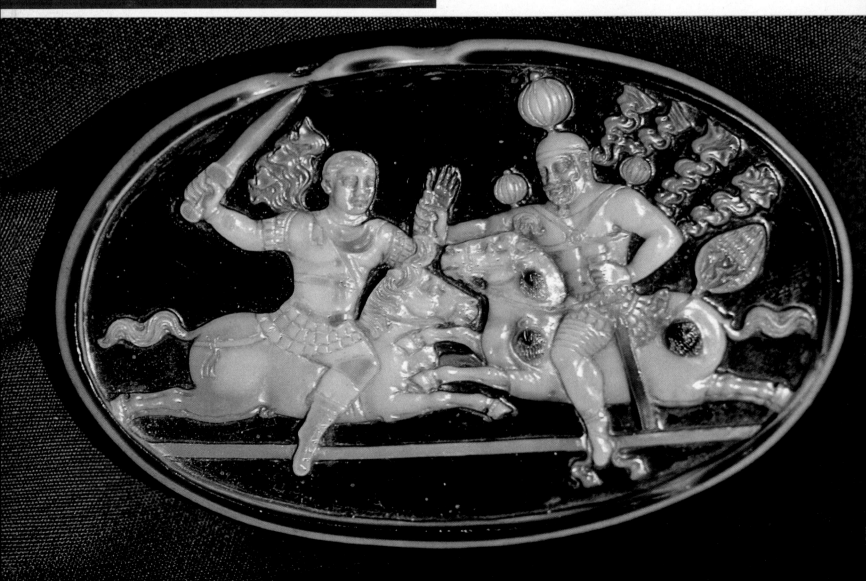

LEFT A recumbent stage modelled in gold for a Scythian shield of the 6th century BC. Most of the early Scythian gold work was functional, concerned with the decoration of their weapons or horse trappings. The curling antlers and the curve of the neck of this stag illustrate something of the exuberant carving and sculptural quality of pre-Hellenistic Scythian work.

The Romans continued to use Greek patterns which they embellished with stones. They also made considerable developments in glass making and cameo carving.

LEFT An example of Roman cameo carving in onyx. This fourth century AD cameo depicts the capture of the Emperor Valerian by Shapur I of Persia in 260 AD. The drama and movement of the scene has been skillfully depicted by the cameo cutter on a tiny scale.

RIGHT A Roman glass and gold necklace. The multi-coloured glass has an iridescent quality due to many centuries burial in the earth. The gold setting appears to be much later, for the wire is of uniform thickness, indicating that it was drawn through a drawplate. Gold wire in the classical era was made by rubbing thin strips of metal between two plates of stone or bronze till it was round; this method naturally produced wire of inconsistent thickness.

THE 'DARK' AGES

LEFT A Frankish strap buckle of the 6th century AD. Frankish jewelry was similar to Anglo Saxon and that of other immigrant tribes who settled in Europe. Jewelry was generally functional, the most common articles being brooches and fibulae, whilst earrings were unknown. This piece is made of gold, silver and niello and decorated with a crude form of filigree, probably adopted from Roman work.

CENTRE The collection of 7th century East Anglian jewelry found in the Sutton Hoo burial is the most outstanding of all medieval work known today. Here is shown one of the two shoulder clasps, gold inlaid with blue and black millefiori glass and garnets. The garnets were cut individually to fit the tiny gold cells or *cloisons*. The technical perfection of this piece would be difficult to achieve today. The design is geometric in the two central panels whilst the border is composed of interlocking abstracted animal forms, similar to Celtic designs.

LEFT A late Anglo Saxon brooch found in the city of London. The central plaque showing a face in cloisonné enamel is framed by gold filigree set with four pearls. Compared with the filigree made 300–400 years earlier, the work is masterly.

BYZANTINE JEWELRY

RIGHT A Byzantine bronze cross embellished with gold leaf and set with a lapis lazuli. Crosses have of course always had a special significance in Christian Europe and jewelers have always devoted their skills to their manufacture. This is an early Christian example.

Saxons were all nomadic warriors who all produced a considerable amount of impressive jewelry.

The leading goldsmiths of this type however were the Scythians, whose period of greatest activity was earlier, contemporary with the Greek civilization. The Scythians were warlike nomads who came from Central Asia and settled on the northern shores of the Caspian sea. They left no heritage of fine architecture, but instead lavished great skill and imagination on the decoration in gold of their personal effects. Most of the excavated Scythian treasures are now in the Hermitage Museum in Leningrad. Like the Greeks, the Scythians used gold almost exclusively. Their designs were naturalistic, and they produced vivid representations of animals full of movement and life. After the conquests of Alexander the Great, they came under Greek influence, and their work adopted a strong Hellenistic flavour.

None of their later successors achieved the same artistic standards, but the jewelers of the Franks, the Goths and Anglo Saxons were clearly very accomplished. The difference in styles between north and south Europe is marked, although everywhere there was an increased use of colour in the form of stones and enamel. The invaders tended to absorb many of the ideas around them; in the north, in England, the Anglo Saxons were influenced by the Celtic designs; whilst in Italy and Spain the Romans use of coarse filigree and granulation was copied. The Anglo Saxon and Frankish jewelers were extremely skilled in stone cutting and cloisonné inlay. It must be explained here that stones were not cut with facets until the 15th century; they were used for their colour, not their optical properties of sparkle and dispersion.

The use of colour in jewelry was as popular in the Byzantine world as in Europe. Byzantine jewelers continued the later Roman patterns and then gradually evolved a new style more closely related to those of the Middle East. Cloisonné enamel was perfected and the gemstones imported from the East to Constantinople were used in profusion. The pierced work known as opus interrasile introduced by the Romans was continued and improved by the Byzantine goldsmiths. ABOVE A pair of seventh century gold opus interassile Byzantine earrings. The crescent shape is typical of Byzantine work.

THE MIDDLE AGES

LEFT The Hildesheim crown. Hildesheim was the cultural centre of the Ottonian empire which was at its height during the eleventh century when this crown was made. The combination of coloured stones and cloisonné enamel shows how much colour was loved at the time. An antique cameo and some antique engraved gems are included amongst the stones. These were thought to possess magical powers and also reflect the admiration for the Romans. Brooches continued to be the most common piece of jewelry until the 15th century when more sophisticated clothes replaced the simple gowns of the middle ages and were accompanied by more elaborate jewelry.

RIGHT A particularly fine 13th century gold ring brooch, set with cabochon rubies and sapphires. The jewelry of this period is rare and mainly ecclesiastical or ceremonial. Secular jewelry was uncommon and simple. Rings, however, remained popular through the middle ages and were based on antique models, until the 13th century, when original designs were introduced.

ABOVE Two fourteenth century gold rings set with sapphires which are examples of these new patterns and show the same simplicity as the gold ring brooch *right*.

17

Two fifteenth century Flemish brooches, made of gold and set with garnets, and in the case of the left brooch, decorated with enamel. Both pieces are highly decorative, with a rich interplay of colour and form, in marked contrast with the simplicity of the previous illustration in the last chapter of two rings made 100 years earlier. Flowers and leaves were again popular decorative motifs.

LEFT A German button in gold and enamel and set with gems; early 17th century.

Little jewelry remains from the four centuries between the Barbarian era and the development of the Renaissance. During this time the Church was at the height of its power, and there was little demand for jewelry. The patrons of the goldsmiths were the Church and Royalty, whose requirements were devotional and ceremonial.

During the 15th century Italy became increasingly prosperous, mainly from her banking and trading activities. A rising middle class gradually gained wealth and power in the towns, the leaders of which such as the Medici family of Florence and the Montefeltro family of Urbino became enthusiastic and energetic patrons of the arts. The climate of thought turned from spirituality to humanism, antiquity became the chief source of inspiration. Classical architectural forms learnt from studying Roman ruins were employed not only in architecture but in painting and sculpture too. This surge of energy in the economic, artistic and philosophical fields is known today as the Renaissance. Goldsmiths were amongst the most respected and admired of the artist craftsmen. Many painters, sculptors and architects trained as goldsmiths, since the training was considered the best for clarity and accuracy in painting. Amongst those who learnt the goldsmith's craft were Brunelleschi, the architect of Florence Cathedral, Verrocchio, the Florentine sculptor, and Botticelli, who used his knowledge of jewelry in many of his pictures, as did Dürer, the German

painter from Nuremberg. Conversely, Holbein the Younger, when court painter to the English King Henry VIII also executed many jewelry designs for Henry who was very much a 'man of the Renaissance' and who delighted in luxury.

Before the Renaissance the importance of piety and spirituality was reflected in women's costume which was plain, simple and concealed the body entirely. In 15th century Italy ideas slowly changed; the body was admired and nudity was sensually portrayed by such painters as Botticelli in his painting 'The birth of Venus'. Similarly clothes became more sumptuous and more revealing, and these changes in fashion allowed for and demanded a profusion of jewelry. During the second half of the 16th century the most exotic and flamboyant jewelry was to be seen at all the European courts and particularly in Spain, Italy, England, France and Germany. During the 16th century Spain was at the height of her power, and the huge gold sources discovered in her South American conquests contributed largely to this. It was Spain that led fashion in Europe during this time, and the clothes of many European courts reflected the wealthy, formal and restrictive life of the Spanish court. Clothes for men and women were elaborate, with high stiff cuffs, big padded sleeves and tight bodices, often made of heavy brocade and inviting a lavish use of jewelry. Both sexes wore pendants, rings, chains and necklaces in profusion.

LEFT This portrait of Sibylla von Freyberg by Bernhard Strigel (1460/61–1528) who was court painter to Emperor Maximillian I shows the more restrained fashions of the late 15th and early 16th century German court. The dress is low necked and high waisted with big flowing sleeves in the Gothic style. However, she wears a huge and complex pendant of gold and enamel which is linked with four chains and set with pearls and gemstones. The pendant has religious significance, a feature of German 16th century jewelry. At the base of the pendant is the Pelican of Piety in a roundel, surmounted by a biblical scene. She holds in her beringed hands a rosary; these were also frequently made by goldsmiths.

RIGHT By the time this portrait of Eleonora Gonzaga, Duchess of Urbino was painted by Titian (1477–1576), the fashion for wearing an abundance of elaborate jewelry was well established. Eleonora Gonzaga is wearing a jeweled chain linked with gold knots, and a pendant, possibly of religious significance, worn on a chain but pinned to her dress. On each wrist is a heavy bracelet set with jewels and on each hand two rings. At this time rings were worn on every finger, including the thumb. Her girdle is gold and from it is suspended a jeweled ermine head, which was believed to provide protection from disease.

FAR RIGHT 'Portrait of a Lady' by Antoine Caron shows the more restricting and austere Spanish style of dress with a high neck and ruff. In this picture the pendant is suspended from both a chain and a jeweled necklace. It is composed of gold, enamelled and set with a cabochon ruby or garnet and emeralds or sapphires. The enamelling too is highly coloured. Two figures of satyrs are also discernible showing the classical influence. The hat is banded with a jeweled chain which matches the necklace. Hat jewels were in common use amongst men and women.

The jewelry of the Renaissance reflects the originality and diversity found in all the arts at the time. The skills of the sculptor, stone setter and enameller were all combined. Classical jewelry, characterized by the use of gold and delicate decorative work, granulation and filigree, was unknown to the 15th century goldsmiths. Entirely new forms were developed which show great classical influence, particularly the sculptural quality of the work and in the use of classical decorative motifs, such as nymphs, satyrs and putti. Mythological subjects like Europa and the Bull and Leda and the Swan are depicted in huge colourful pendants, whilst the taste for fantasy and the exotic is seen in the portrayal of mermen, fantastic beasts, dragons, hippocampi (sea horse monsters) and

griffins. The sculptured gold figures are decorated with brilliant coloured enamel and coloured stones, chiefly rubies and emeralds. Baroque pearls were widely used, either suspended from pendants, brooches or earrings, or incorporated in the figures as part of the body.

Antique cameos and intaglios, depicting classical heads and mythological subjects were chiefly carved in sardonyx or cornelian and were particularly admired. At the beginning of the 16th century jewelers used cameos which had survived from antiquity, but over the years the lapidaries improved and at the end of the century Milan became the centre for intaglio and cameo carving. The art spread through Europe and many portrait cameos and medallions of Elizabeth I survive.

Animals, enamelled and set with stones are common amongst Renaissance pendants. RIGHT are two horses, whose origins are difficult to place for goldsmiths travelled around Europe as did the pattern books. *Right above* is an annunciation pendant, in which the primitive figure modelling and delicate gold work suggest English manufacture. BELOW The pendant representing St George and the Dragon is possibly also English.

Bird pendants, such as parrots, pelicans, swans and eagles were made all over Europe but eagles set with emeralds are particularly associated with Spain. LEFT A Spanish eagle of the late 16th century set with a huge garnet cabochon.

Pendant jewels designed as ships as BELOW can reasonably be attributed to a Venetian craftsman. These two are late 16th century but substantial and well-made. The ship on the right shows the characteristic 16th century habit of incorporating baroque pearls into the design. Ships of more flimsy workmanship often decorated with quantities of seed pearls are generally associated with Southern Italy.

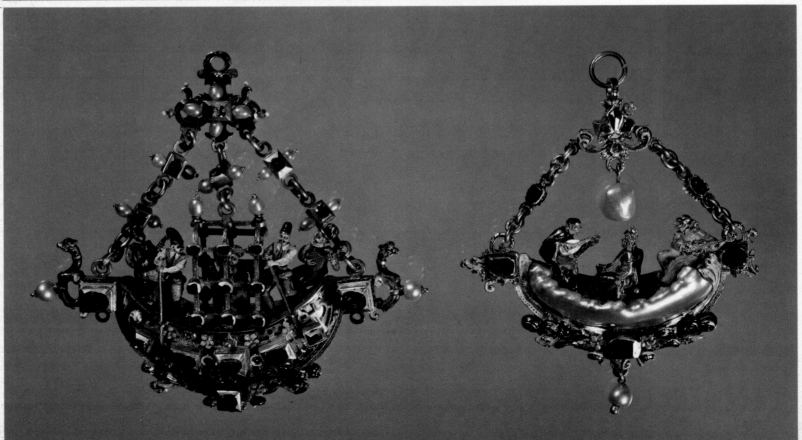

ABOVE An early 17th century German button, which still shows most of the characteristic features of 16th century work: the multicoloured enamel, the rubies and pearls and the figure. But it is no longer classical in inspiration, the figure is not classical and the decoration is naturalistic, without any scrolls or putti—in fact it is indicative of the changes to come in jewelry design during the 17th century. A relatively large proportion of 16th century jewelry survives but only rarely comes on the market, commanding extremely high prices when it does.

Roman cameos were highly valued during the 15th and 16th centuries, although contemporary lapidaries were improving their techniques, so that during the 16th century beautifully carved onyx cameos and engraved gems were being produced in Italy and later in France and England. LEFT A very fine carving of Cosimo de Medici and his family, executed by the Florentine de Rossi.

RIGHT Mary Tudor painted by Antonio Moro. This was probably a wedding portrait and shows the more severe, Northern taste, although her tight bodiced dress with sleeves and high neck follows the Spanish style. Whilst like Eleonora Gonzaga she wears a jeweled pendant suspended from a jeweled necklace, she also wears a bracelet on each arm, a jeweled girdle and several rings. Her hat, dress and gloves are decorated with jewels as well.

25

The exuberant luxury of the 16th century did not continue far into the 17th century; all over Europe the flamboyant taste for the exotic and fantastic gave way to a cooler more elegant style. It was a century of wars; the thirty years war crippled Europe, whilst in England civil war resulted in Puritan rule for 20 years under Oliver Cromwell. The Dutch Netherlands, however were at the height of their power and creativity. It was largely through the widespread Dutch trading links that oriental goods such as silks, porcelain, spices and plants reached Europe, whilst at home it was at this time that Rembrandt, Vermeer, Van Ruisdael and Frans Hals were painting. But Holland was a protestant country, its power was in the hands of merchants and burghers who preferred sober restraint to the lavish extravagance which had been seen in the 15th century Spanish court (which was to be seen again at the French court of Versailles 100 years later). All these things contributed to the fact that little jewelry was made or has survived from the 17th century. Jewelry and plate were melted down to pay for arms, whilst the protestant outlook discouraged vanity or extravagance.

Towards the end of the century things changed. Louis XIV ascended the French throne, and Charles II was restored to the English throne. A new era had begun, with France as the centre of fashion. This was to continue until the French Revolution of 1789, the event that shook Europe, radically affecting many aspects of life including the making of jewelry.

During the 17th century there was a growing interest in the sciences, including botany; at the same time naturalism came into fashion, and flowers, including the new oriental varieties, were extremely popular in all areas of design. They were used particularly in embroidery, textiles, marquetry and carving in furniture, and in jewelry. During the 1630s tulip mania emanating from Holland was at its height.

Costume also changed considerably. The stiff Spanish ruffs, tight bodices, and huge farthingales gave way to softer lines and softer fabrics; damasks, silks, and lace replaced heavy brocades, and low necklines replaced high ones. A more sensual feminity took the place of formality and courtliness. In jewelry design, styles also changed radically. The brilliant polychromy of renaissance enamel was replaced by paler and later, single colours. The sculptured three dimensional work gave way to flat enamelled and stone-set work. Figures disappeared entirely, whilst flower patterns and designs evolved from naturalistic forms replaced them. Gold was used less and less as a decorative feature, until in the 18th century it was only used for settings to secure the stones.

Having described some of the many changes in design, it is important to say here that new fashions in jewelry never occur fast, often passing through long transitional stages, with elements of the new and the old designs together. It is only possible to talk about Renaissance styles, protestant eras, and 18th century elegance within roughly defined time spans, there were no sudden changes

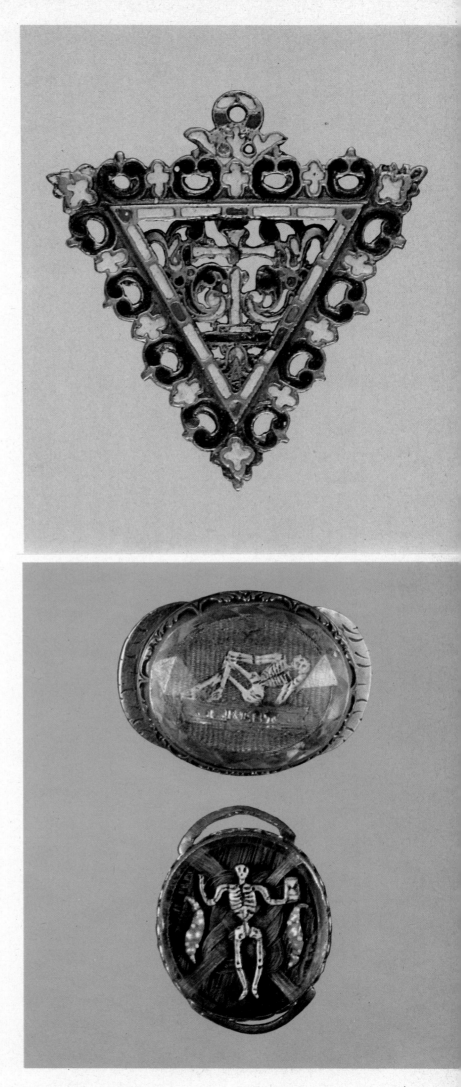

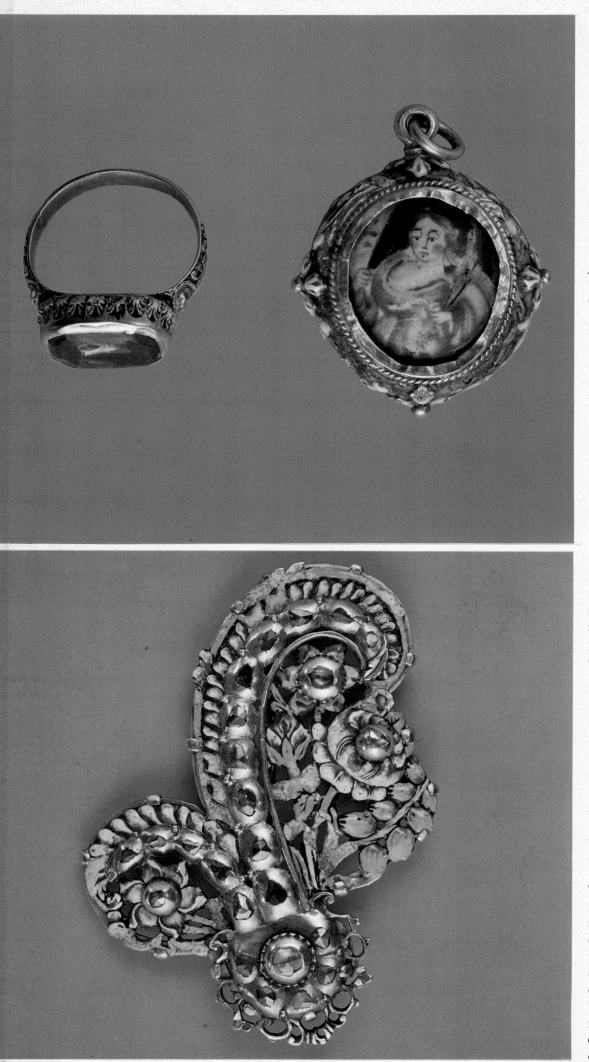

PREVIOUS PAGES
During the 17th century, the brilliant colours of 16th century enamel were replaced by more restrained tones. TOP shows a heavily enamelled devotional pendant in white and blue, typical colours of the period. It is flat in comparison with the sculptural three dimensional quality of 16th century pieces. The workmanship on this piece is not exceptional and the pendant was apparently for everyday use.

Reliquary jewelry was made all over Europe but mourning jewelry was an English peculiarity. The early mourning jewelry in England was made in the 17th century and had a somewhat sinister quality. BELOW are two Stuart slides with enamelled skeletons set under crystal. One is flanked by two fishes, whilst the other has the motto 'Rest'. Mourning rings of this period often include white enamelled skulls set with diamond eyes.

LEFT An Italian, 17th century enamelled ring, set with a step cut ameythyst circa 1630. Lapidary methods were improving throughout the 17th century and stones began to be used for their optical properties of reflection and refraction, rather than for their colour. By the late 17th century, amethysts had lost popularity. The enamel design has been painted on this ring and is in very good condition. Enamel, being a vitreous substance, chips easily and is difficult to repair. On the *right* is a Spanish reliquary pendant of gold and painted enamel circa 1630.

LEFT Enseigne or hat feather brooch. The front and reverse of this piece are thickly enamelled in bright colours of pink, red, purple, yellow and green. The rough cut diamonds are set in solid backed silver settings and having no sparkle, resemble glass. Such pieces were worn in hats, usually by men and they are rare. The enamelled flowers illustrate the popular liking for plants and gardens which was widespread in the 17th century.

The passion for flowers is also illustrated RIGHT in a very fine diamond and silver pendant of English manufacture during the early 18th century. This pendant incorporates three of the most common motifs of the late 17th and 18th centuries; a bow, a cross and flowers. The diamonds are rose cut, reflecting more light and sparkle than those of the enseigne. The silver is used for the settings only and not for decoration.

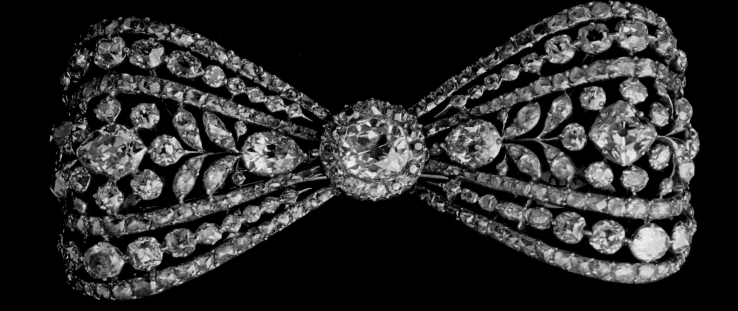

ABOVE Compare this piece with the previous pendant. It is a beautifully made English brooch of the mid 18th century, and the silver is hardly visible at all. The floral decoration is secondary to the bow design. The diamonds have the relatively new brilliant cut, but the settings are still solid backed. Open backed settings were not introduced until around 1770. It is possible that this brooch was part of a set with two or three identical but smaller ones which were worn on the V shaped stomacher of 18th century dress bodices.

The trend for softer, less restricting dresses in the 17th century inevitably excluded the high Spanish ruff. It was abandoned and replaced by low necklines, which allowed women to wear earrings. Drop pearl earrings were never out of favour and pearls were particularly popular during the 17th century, but towards the end of the century earrings of all kinds had become an important item of jewelry. As hair styles became more outrageous in the 18th century, earrings became larger and larger to balance the huge coiffures and could be as much as three inches wide. RIGHT A pair of mid-eighteenth century Spanish earrings set with emeralds. This style of earring with three or five pear-shaped or round suspended pendants is known as 'Girandole' and was extremely popular for pendants and brooches as well as earrings. The Spanish continued to use emeralds more than any other country. LEFT Another pair of mid 18th century Spanish earrings of chrysolite set in silver and gold. Here the design and workmanship is much more elegant.

at any point and the speed at which fashions in life styles altered varied enormously from country to country and from town to town. The jewelry described as typical of the Renaissance or of the 18th century is that which has emerged as the most distinctive in style and the most representative of the characteristic of the period at its height. Old styles often continue to be used in one country long after they have been superseded in another. For example Renaissance styles continued to be used in Hungary throughout the 17th and 18th centuries, Spain too, continued the styles of the previous era during the 17th century.

Miniatures were very popular at this period, often mounted in jeweled frames, watches too were highly sought after, also mounted in jeweled cases. The flat and slightly rounded surfaces of these cases were particularly suitable for enamelling, and many had coloured flowers painted in enamel on monochromic backgrounds, or flower and scroll designs in champlevé enamel. Pale blue on a white ground was amongst the most common combination of colours. The best work of this kind was done in France and the Low Countries. Even in pieces such as pendants and brooches which were dominated by stones, the surrounding decorative gold scroll work was picked out in enamel, the reverse side too was enamelled,

often with flowers. However towards the end of the century enamel work decoration declined, and eventually disappeared.

Throughout the 17th century stone cutting improved; the rose cut was developed which made more use of the reflective and sparkling properties of gemstones, whereas previously stones had been used for the colour alone. Accordingly, stones became an increasingly important feature. The most significant development in jewelry at this time was the improved understanding of lapidary work, and the optical properties of gems. It is possible that techniques were introduced from India, where the huge deposits of diamonds and emeralds were being exploited by the Moghul rulers, and exported to the west. About 1700 a major innovation was made with the *brilliant cut* which is still the most usual cut for diamonds. Its 58 facets revealed for the first time the hitherto unexploited properties of gemstones, that is, to refract and reflect light creating a multicoloured sparkle, qualities which lay hidden by the unfaceted cabochon stone and barely touched by the cruder rose cut. From this moment diamonds became the most important and most prized feature of jewelry for the next hundred years, indeed they have maintained their attraction and fascination to the present day.

LEFT Two stomacher brooches. The one *left* is composed of rubies, emeralds and sapphires set in gold and is not typical of the period which favoured diamonds and pale coloured stones, such as the topaz in the brooch *below*. The setting of the rubies, emeralds and sapphires is not of a very high standard, whilst the design in unbalanced and heavy. This could denote middle European or Russian origins. The topaz brooch is more elegantly made, although the stones do not appear to match well in colour. This is partly due to the foils which were placed behind the stones to improve their colour, and in this case, some of the settings have allowed in air or water which damages the foils. The simplicity of the topaz piece suggests English origins.

Another popular stone during the 18th and early 19th centuries was the garnet. They were flat cut and set in solid backed settings. BELOW LEFT An English garnet necklace set in silver of the mid eighteenth century shows this use of flat cut garnets. The necklace has terminal loops at either end instead of a clasp. This is because 18th century necklaces were fastened with a piece of ribbon passed through each loop and tied in a bow at the back of the neck. Jewelry tended to be worn in the evening only, ribbons and real flowers were worn during the daytime. The necklace is composed of symmetrical flowers alternating with asymmetrical ribbon and bud designs, which show the influence of the rococo style.

RIGHT Garnet aigrette or hair ornament, circa 1780. Hair ornaments were very popular, often in the form of feathers or ears of wheat. The three arms of this spray quiver when the piece is worn.

Yellow gold was felt to detract from the cool blue white colour of diamonds, so silver became the favourite setting metal. Meanwhile an important discovery was made in glass making. In the 1770s George Ravenscroft developed a new strong dense glass with the use of lead. The new lead glass had many of the properties of diamonds when faceted as if it were a gemstone. It reflected and refracted light well, glittering with many different colours. These glass stones are known as paste, or strass after George Frederic Strass who was jeweler to the king of France for twenty years, (1734–1754) and did much to promote paste jewelry among the higher echelons of society as well as among the less wealthy. Jewelers set diamonds and paste alike, consequently the designs and craftsmanship of paste jewels are of the same quality as their more expensive counterparts. Paste jewelry has survived the test of time rather better than diamond pieces, because the small value of the glass stones has protected it from being broken up and remodelled into new styles. Perhaps the most distinctive feature of paste is that it can be cut into any shape to fit a design, whereas diamonds are too precious and too hard to be treated in this way.

The most important items of jewelry from the mid 1400s to the late 18th century were necklaces, stomachers (an unappealing term for the brooches often worn in sets of three or five down the V shaped stomacher or front of the bodice) and earrings which reached vast dimensions, sometimes two and a half to three inches wide. Rings were always favoured whilst aigrettes or hair ornaments grew in popularity during the 18th century as hair styles became increasingly elaborate. They were most often in the form of ears of wheat or stylized feathers. Flowers remained a popular design motif, which became lighter and more delicate. During the 1720s the rococo style characterized by asymmetrical forms lightness, feminity and gaiety emanated from France. The asymmetry and the more open quality of mid 18th century pieces is in sharp contrast to the heavier and symmetrical designs of earlier work. Bows were a very popular motif used in brooches and necklaces, and were mixed with floral and naturalistic designs. Necklaces were fastened not with a snap, but with a piece of ribbon passed through the terminal loops at either end of the necklace, and tied in a bow at the back of the neck. Necklaces, earrings and brooches were made in the same design as a set, known as a *parure*, whereas previously each piece was made separately.

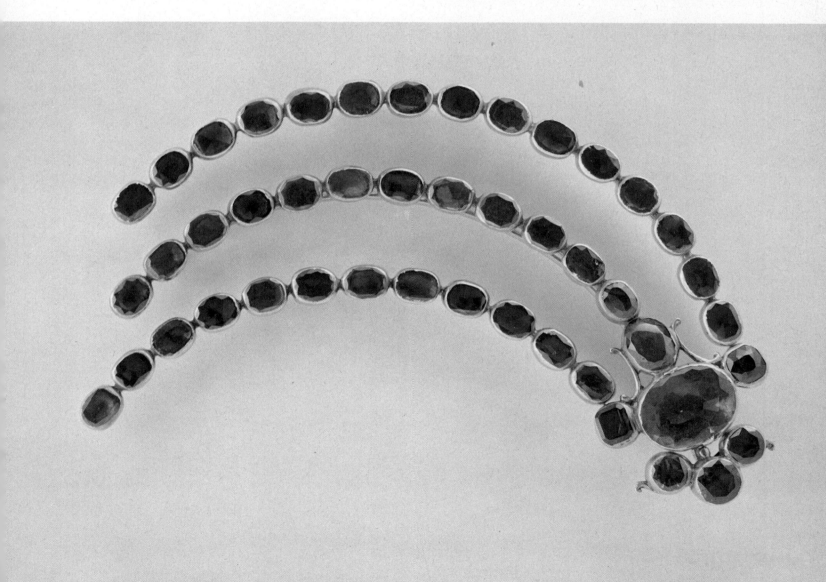

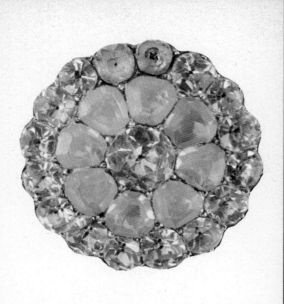

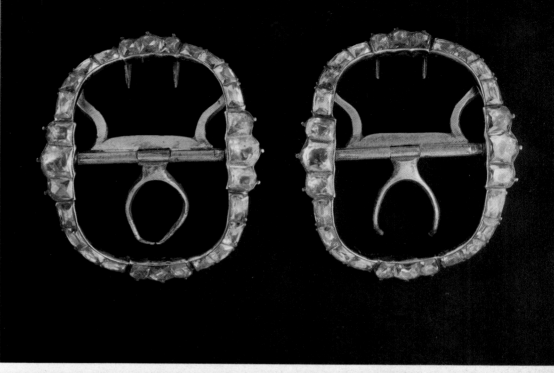

RIGHT Another aigrette in the form of a feather set with fine rose cut diamonds. This is probably slightly earlier than the garnet piece, and its rather heavy and compact look is typical of English Georgian jewelry. It is beautifully made and has been adapted as a brooch.

Jewelry had become the prerogative of women during the 17th century; the only jeweled ornaments worn by men were finger rings, buttons and buckles. Jeweled orders and decorations worn at court were the exception to this rule. Considerable skill, imagination and money were spent on buckles and buttons. Louix XIV, for example, owned two diamond parures with 171 diamond buttons in one and 216 in the other. Men wore not only shoe buckles but buckles at the knee, the cuff and the waist. They were set with precious stones, paste and marcasite; they were enamelled on plain silver, steel or pinchbeck. ABOVE RIGHT A pair of silver shoe buckles set with topaz which date from the late 18th century.

Buttons too were the subject of the jeweler's skill. One French nobleman is known to have worn a set of diamond buttons, each of which encased a miniature watch. France and England were the major button centres, though button production in the United States grew during the 18th century. They were made in sets from 5 to 35. Paste was a popular material. LEFT AND TOP Four buttons from a set made of clear and opaline paste. Generally, coloured paste stones bear little resemblance to their natural stone counterparts, opaline and clear paste are the exceptions.

35

After the Renaissance jewelry became the perogative of women, and male jewelry was limited to buttons, buckles and rings, although all these were treated as items of value, made with diamonds and other precious stones for the very rich and with paste, garnets or cut steel for the less fortunate.

The feeling of the rococo style and also evidence of the delight in discovery of the brilliant cut was illustrated by the habit of 18th century women of wearing jewelry almost exclusively in the evening, when the stones sparkled in the candlelight, and were reflected in the many mirrors which were an essential item of 18th century interior decoration. During the daytime very little jewelry was worn, instead real flowers and ribbons were fastened at the neck, and at the breast.

During the 17th century there was wide and enthusiastic interest in the Sciences which was reflected in the taste for clocks and watches. The watches were often encased in jeweled frames.

LEFT AND TOP Five mid 18th century French watch cases. The *top left* case is of banded agate, and has a rococo frame of pierced and chased gold. *Above* is a painted enamel case, probably the earliest piece. *Centre* is an enamelled gold case set with pearls, rubies, diamonds and peridots. *Below and right* are chased gold cases; the one *below* depicts a classical scene.

The chatelaines which supported these watches were no less fine. They were hooked to a belt at the waist, and from them were suspended not only watches but also miniatures, pomanders and étuis, three of which are illustrated. RIGHT *top left* Chased gold Dutch étui circa 1755 containing a spoon, a fork and scissors. *Top right* Chased gold German étui circa 1720 containing a spoon and fork, scissors and sugar tongs. *Below right* Gold étui set with carved cornelians, English, circa 1720, containing a spoon, scissors and pencils. They often held an assortment of sewing and drawing instruments such as thimbles, rulers and compasses.

Late 18th century chatelaines and étuis are still available, often in pinchbeck, cut steel or marcasite. 18th century jewelry is not very plentiful now, since many pieces have been broken up and reset or adapted. Paste has survived better because its intrinsic value is too low to merit resetting but prices are high now.

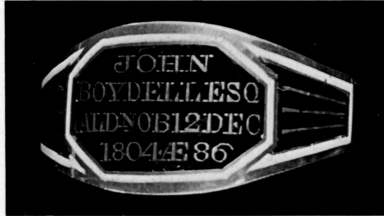

In the last quarter of the 18th century, two important events occurred. One was the French Revolution of 1789 and the other, a more gradual development, was the beginning of the Industrial Revolution. Both these factors influenced the development and appearance of jewelry.

During the years leading up to the French Revolution there had been a growing interest in the study of Greek thought and in the strict rules of Greek architecture. The French revolutionaries liked to think of themselves as citizens of a new Athens, the newly independent Americans chose to build Washington along strictly classical lines, whilst the new town of Edinburgh was called the Athens of the North. The old elaborate styles of baroque and rococo were identified with the *ancien regime* and rejected, whilst the influence of the classical revival permeated all fields of art and design including clothes and jewelry. At the same time, from the mid 18th century industry was growing and crafts were becoming increasingly mechanized. The middle classes, which were also growing with the increasing prosperity started a demand for articles such as jewelry which in consequence led to the beginnings of cheap mass production.

For more than a decade after the French Revolution, it was extremely unwise to wear any diamond jewelry in Paris, since it was strongly associated with the *ancien regime*. Many of the French jewelers fled to London where society had never reached the extremes of extravagance enjoyed by the pre-Revolutionary French aristocracy, and where the diamond mounter could still find employment. However when Napoleon was crowned emperor, the call for jewelry was again established in France, and Paris was restored to its position as the fashion leader of Europe.

The look of jewelry changed considerably during the late 18th century. The massive earrings, stomachers and brooches were replaced with smaller earrings, necklaces and brooches which were worn with the simple, new high-waisted dresses. Diamonds lost popularity, whilst less

The source of inspiration for all areas of the arts during the Grecian revival was classical antiquity. Engraved gems and cameos returned to favour, whilst new forms and imitations of portrait medallions were introduced.

ABOVE A marquise-shaped brooch of enamelled silver set with fine rose cut diamonds, which illustrates the taste for simplicity in the 1770s and '80s.

James Tassie pioneered a technique of mass produced moulded glass cameos, the simplicity of which is again typical of the period.

LEFT A Tassie memorial portrait cameo in glass of the methodist preacher, John Wesley (1703–91). Cameos depicting blackamoors were also popular. RIGHT A French 'blackamoor' chatelaine circa 1795 set with cameos, rubies and diamonds.

40

During the last three decades of the 18th century the taste for luxury and elaborate ornamentation which emanated from pre-revolutionary France was replaced by the cool restraint of neoclassicism. This is illustrated most clearly in English mourning jewelry.

PREVIOUS PAGES

LEFT An English mourning brooch of enamelled gold set with tiny diamonds and pearls framing a carved ivory urn with flowers, circa 1780. The restrained approach is evident: the simple oval outline replaces the asymmetry of the rococo designs, whilst ivory, enamel and pearls take the place of sparkling diamonds.

PAGE 39

TOP LEFT Two painted enamel mourning pendants flank an enamelled pinchbeck buckle. The pendants are typical of the styles at the end of the 18th century, when sentiment softened the austerity of earlier neoclassicism. Many mourning rings, pendants and brooches depict mourning widows in classical dress lamenting by a classical urn. Weeping willow trees, buds of peace and angels are frequently included in the scene. The pendant on the right has a frame of plaited hair. The central buckle is beautifully enamelled and is a collector's item. It is not difficult to tell pinchbeck from gold when the two are compared side by side, pinchbeck tarnishes whilst gold never loses its shine. Sometimes pinchbeck is washed with gold but a tiny scratch will reveal the pinchbeck under the plated surface.

TOP RIGHT A mourning ring circa 1780 with a classical urn of enamelled gold set with diamonds on a mother of pearl background in a blue enamelled frame. The marquise-shaped frame is typical of the late 18th and early 19th century.

CENTRE is a simpler mourning ring enamelled in black with the name of the deceased, John Boydell, on it and the date of his death at the age of 86 on 12th December 1804. It was common for a gentleman to bequeath a sum of money for a set of mourning rings to be made and then distributed to his friends and family. White enamelled rings of this type generally commemorated a child or young girl.

BELOW This English memorial pendant of the late 18th century is more elaborate. The central spray is made of hair set with pearls and diamonds and the frame is of red enamel and fine rose cut diamonds.

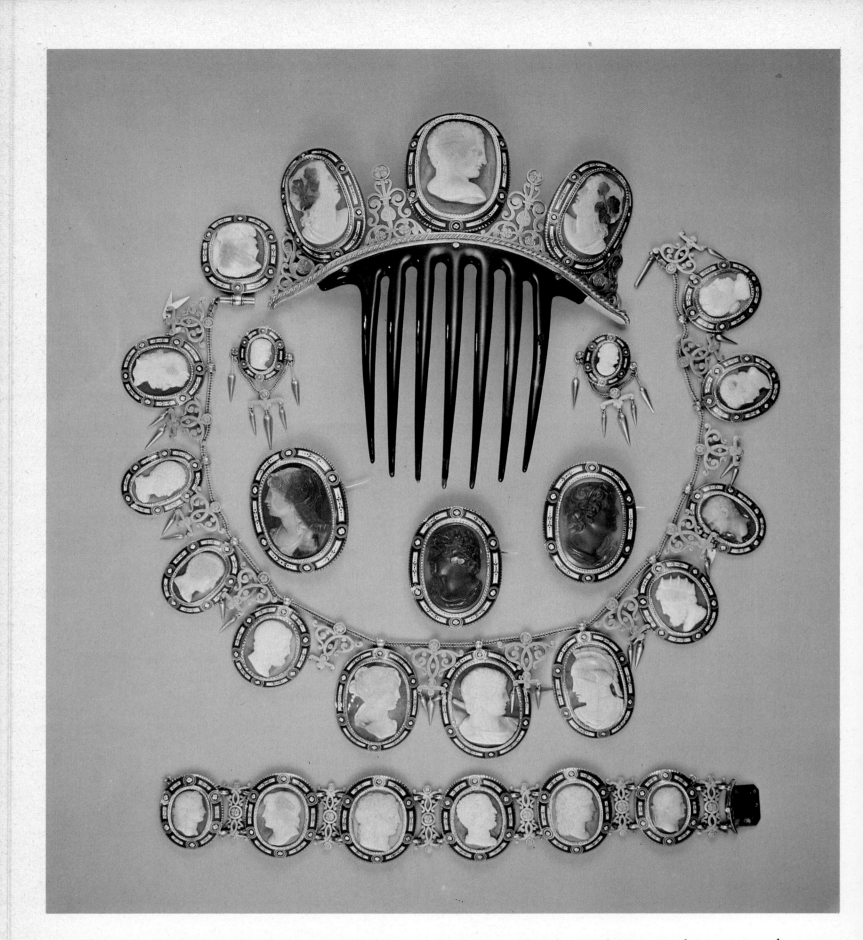

valuable and less brilliantly glittering materials took their place. Garnets, amber, cornelian and moss agate became fashionable. Cameos were enormously popular; the Empress Josephine, who loved all jewelry, persuaded Napoleon to remove some antique cameos from the Bibliotheque Nationale and to have them set. Cameos made at that time were mounted on rings, necklaces, brooches and tiaras, and imitation cameos were made in a wide variety of materials. Originally cameos were cut

in stone. Onyx or sardonyx was the most popular stone, although emeralds, amethysts were also widely used, and at the beginning of the 19th century shell cameos were introduced in Italy. Josiah Wedgwood produced quantities of jasperware cameos in a wide variety of shapes and colours, decorated with white figures and patterns which were then used for rings, brooches, earrings, bracelets and buttons, generally set in mounts of pinchbeck or cut steel. Miniature painters produced paintings *en grisaille*, with

After Napoleon's victories, the classical style captivated the French, the pomp of Rome replaced the simplicity of Greece and prevailed during the First French Empire. Technical perfection was the goal of jewelers and engravers. Parures of cameos were worn for evening and even during the day. Shell cameos were introduced from Naples and southern Italy. The Empress Josephine had the antique cameos in the national collection of the Biblioteque Nationale set into a parure for herself.

LEFT A cameo parure in gold and enamelled settings of exquisite workmanship. Cameos remained popular throughout the 19th century but became more ornate and elaborate.

Josiah Wedgwood produced classical plaques in blue and white and black and white basalt ware. These were often set in pinchbeck or cut steel frames.

RIGHT Two bracelets of blue, black and white 18th century wedgwood sections connected by gold chain. They can be joined to form a necklace. This piece was made later and signed by Carlo Giuliano in the mid 1800s.

FOLLOWING PAGE
An English aigrette of pearls and diamonds. The crescent set with pearls and diamonds is a later addition. The symmetry of the piece contrasts with the asymmetry of the two earlier aigrettes illustrated on pages 33 and 35, whilst the diamond-set star is typical of the turn of the century. Star brooches were very popular at that time.

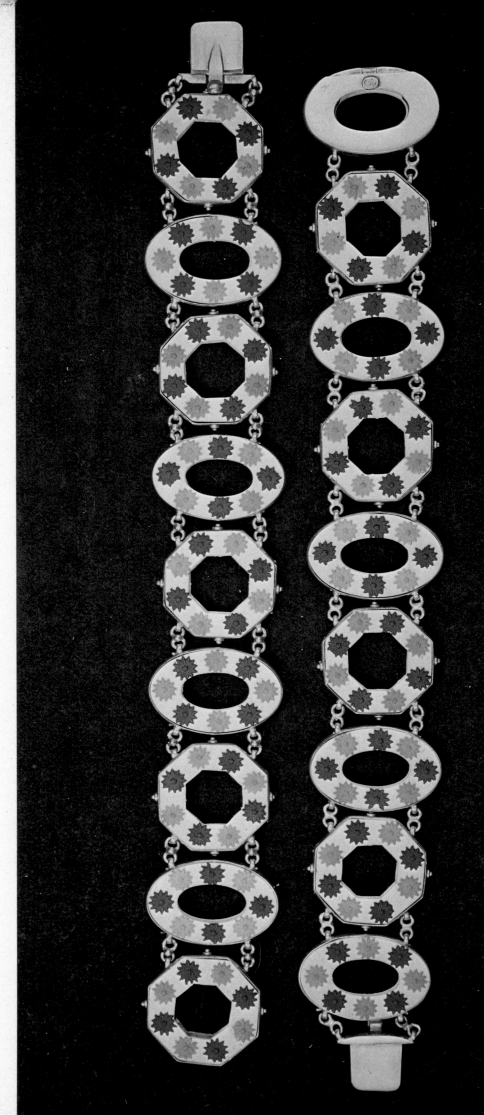

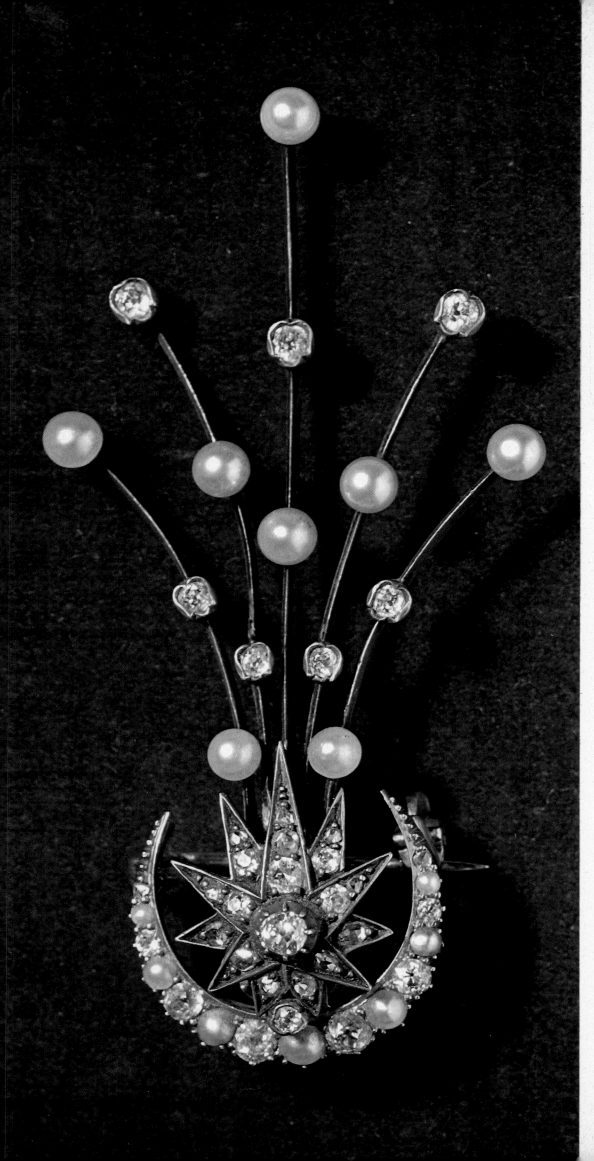

One of the effects of the Industrial Revolution was the increased production of cut steel jewelry by Matthew Boulton in Birmingham. Cut steel had been made at Woodstock since the 17th century but gained in popularity during the 18th century due to its similarity to cut stones. It was made by faceting and polishing stone and bears a close resemblance to marcasite. The difference is easily discerned by examining the reverse side. Marcasite is set in settings in the same way as stones, whilst cut steel is riveted to the setting from the back, and the rivet heads are clearly visible on the reverse.

RIGHT A pair of late 18th century earrings and buckles.

Another form of jewelry to emerge from the new industrialization was Berlin Iron. This delicate, cast iron jewelry was the speciality of the Prussian Royal Iron foundry in Berlin. Although production started at the beginning of the 19th century, it was not till the Prussian war of liberation against Napoleon (1813–15) that its popularity grew. German patriots contributed to the war effort by exchanging their valuable jewelry for iron replicas. ABOVE A fine Berlin Iron necklace and brooch. Unfortunately little has survived since it is extremely brittle and not intrinsically valuable, consequently much was destroyed after the vogue passed in the 1830s.

backgrounds of blue or sepia, which were then set in clasps and pendants, James Tassie produced imitation intaglios in glass, engraved with figures and scenes copied from famous intaglio collections and from paintings; these were generally set in seals and worn on fob chains by men.

Pearls have rarely been out of fashion, but during the 18th century they did lose favour, returning to popularity at the end of the century. They were used in necklaces, and also to surround other stones.

The classical influence is clearly seen in late 18th and early 19th century mourning jewelry. Mourning jewelry was peculiar to England, dating back to the 17th century when many memorial rings commemorating Charles I were made at the restoration of Charles II in 1660. By the second half of the 18th century mourning jewelry had become widespread and had lost the somewhat macabre quality of earlier fashions. Weeping ladies were depicted mourning by urns under weeping willow trees in painted enamel or oval or marquise shaped plaques, which were then set in rings and pendants surrounded by pearls, marcasites, rose diamond or enamel. Sometimes a lock of hair from the deceased was incorporated and it was common practice for a man to bequeath a sum of money for rings which his family and friends should wear

in his memory. These rings are generally of black or blue enamel with the name and dates of the departed in gold letters, white examples of this type are usually to commemorate a child or young girl. The mourning jewelry illustrates another aspect of the late 18th century taste— sentimentality—this is also seen in French work where devices such as hearts, bows and arrows and other amorous symbols are employed.

Wedgwood's jasperware cameos were one example of the new, cheap, mass produced forms of jewelry, pinchbeck and cut steel pieces are two more examples. Pinchbeck is an alloy of zinc and copper and was introduced by Christopher Pinchbeck in the early 18th century to imitate gold. In the 19th century it was used chiefly for mounts. Cut steel was taken up and developed by Matthew Boulton in Birmingham. Steel was faceted and highly polished to resemble cut stones, it was used for buckles, chatelaines, necklaces, earrings and bracelets. Chatelaines had been introduced in the early 18th century, but their popularity continued. They were worn by women and attached to a belt at the waist, and from their three or five chains were suspended keys, étuis or boxes holding sewing tools, miniatures, pomanders and other similar small objects.

LEFT Madame de Senonnes painted by Ingres, wearing an early 19th century empire line dress. On her fingers are twelve little rings mostly set with one stone, amongst them, several garnet rings which were still popular. Round her neck are two lockets and a cross suspended from long chains, and she has drop earrings set with rubies or garnets in her ears, and finally a tiara barely visible in her hair. Tiaras came into fashion with the classical revival and remained *de rigueur* for court dress until after the First World War. A more complex cross than that of Mme de Senonnes is shown RIGHT. It is composed of garnets and diamonds. The plain outline of the cross shows the taste for simplicity circa 1800, whilst the floral spray which surmounts it is in the earlier 18th century style.

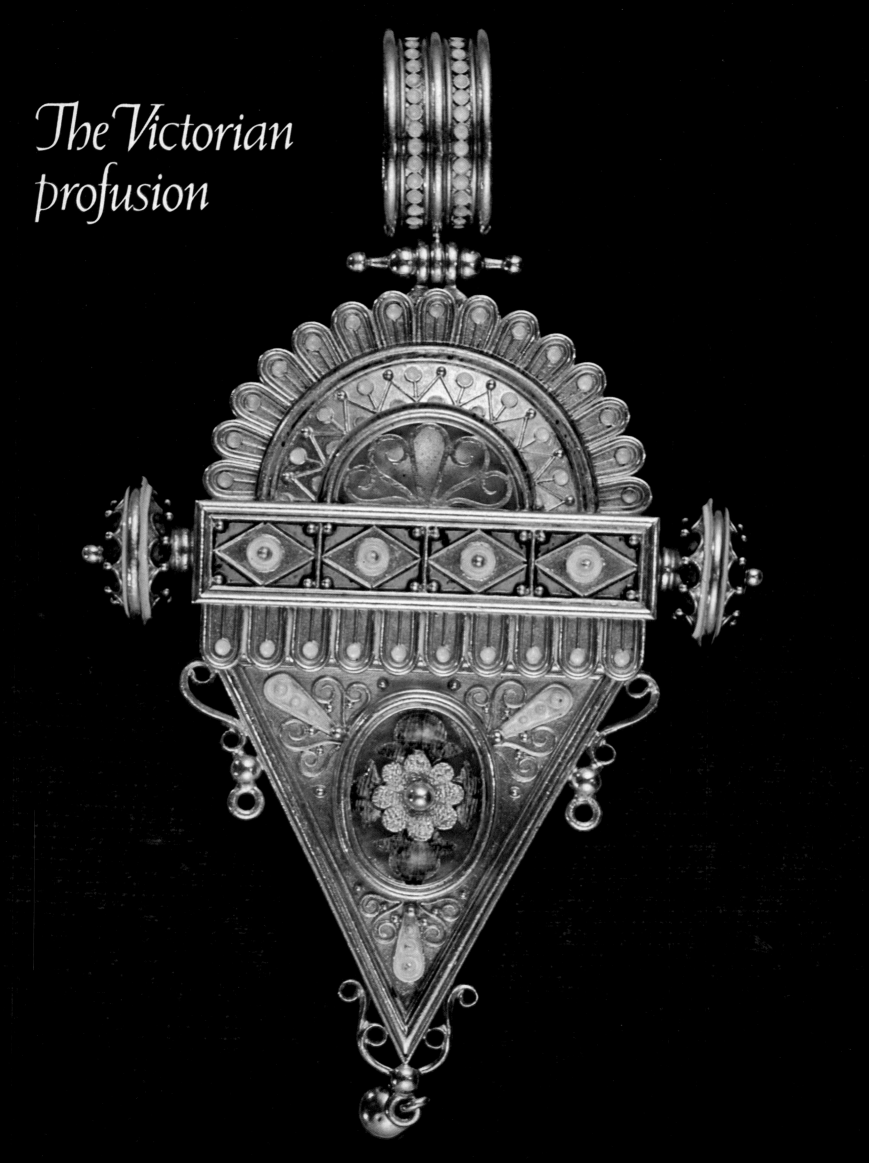

The Victorian profusion

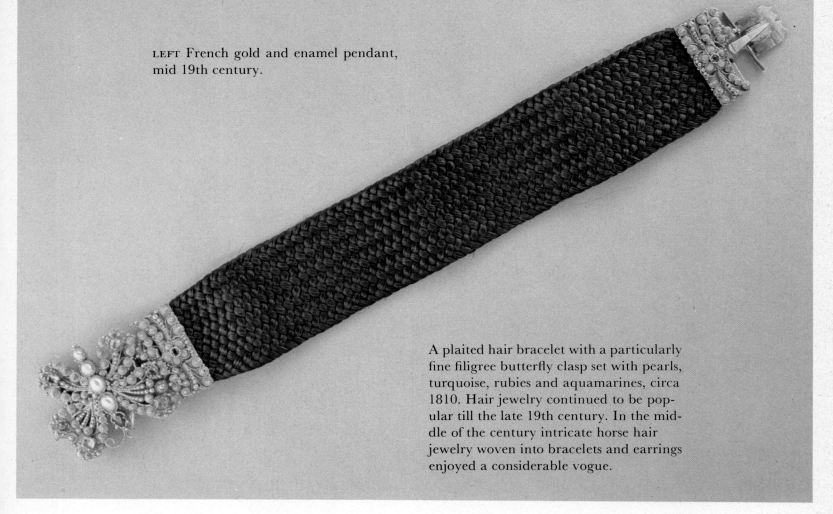

LEFT French gold and enamel pendant, mid 19th century.

A plaited hair bracelet with a particularly fine filigree butterfly clasp set with pearls, turquoise, rubies and aquamarines, circa 1810. Hair jewelry continued to be popular till the late 19th century. In the middle of the century intricate horse hair jewelry woven into bracelets and earrings enjoyed a considerable vogue.

Like all the applied arts in the 19th century, jewelry is characterized by profusion and the variety of designs, techniques, materials and forms. The expansion of industry continued, and new techniques and materials were constantly being introduced. Owing to mass production more jewelry was produced than ever before, and it ceased to be the perogative of the wealthy classes. Pieces were stamped out of thin gold sheet decorated with filigree, (a technique known as Cannetille) and set with brightly coloured stones, such as pink and yellow topaz. Or they were made with pinchbeck and set with pastes in imitation of expensive work. Carved ivory, jet, and piqué work, which is ivory or tortoiseshell inlaid with gold studs, are amongst inexpensive ideas which were developed. Because of the quantity of jewelry produced during the 19th century much of it is available today to the collector at reasonable prices. Most Victorian design was derivative, and all the previous styles were called on, the Gothic, Renaissance, Classical and Baroque were all readapted.

When Queen Victoria ascended the throne in 1837 the romantic period was in full swing. The novels of Walter Scott and Victor Hugo generated an intense interest in historical knowledge which spread to dress and jewelry designs. The interest in medievalism lasted throughout the century, but was particularly intense at this time. For example, a tournament followed by a medieval ball was proposed to celebrate the coronation of the Queen. Jewelry designs were taken from 16th century work, as portrayed in portraits and engravings and surviving originals, since a relatively large amount of renaissance jewelry survived the test of time. Around the middle of the century and later, direct copies were made, (prior to that 16th century ideas had been adapted). However, 19th century pieces can generally be distinguished from the originals by their superior enamelling in less brilliant colours. Reproductions of the Greco-Roman pieces excavated in the Mediterranean enjoyed considerable popularity, and again can be distinguished from the originals by their superior craftsmanship. From the 1820s till the 1840s cannetille of different coloured golds, set with pink or yellow topaz were particularly popular in England, though found in France and Switzerland too. This taste for soft muted colours gave way to a more ostentatious flamboyance around the middle of the century both in England and in France where the lavish court of the Second Empire dominated fashion. Huge pieces came into vogue such as wide cuff-like bracelets set with huge brilliantly coloured stones; amethysts and garnet cabochons being amongst the most popular. This bold jewelry suited the wide crinolines of the 1860s. Towards the end of the century an element of restraint was introduced. The strong colours of jewelry and dress were replaced with more sober tones. Diamonds and pearls, silver, ivory and amber came into favour. The discovery in 1867 of the diamond deposits in South Africa led to a sharp increase in the production of diamonds.

LEFT Grigoletti portrait of a lady which shows the dress of the 1830s. It was fashionable in the 1830s to wear a pendant or *ferroniere* on the forehead in the manner of the blacksmith's wife in Leonardo da Vinci's portrait 'La belle ferroniere'. This reflected the romantic interest in medievalism.

RIGHT A gold and enamel necklace set with rubies, turquoise and pearls circa 1840. Although this necklace was made with contemporary cannetille techniques of mass production, each unit being stamped out of thin gold, the renaissance style enamel work reflects the romantic nostalgic feeling of the time. The soft muted tones of pearls and turquoise were particularly popular from the 1820s to the middle of the century.

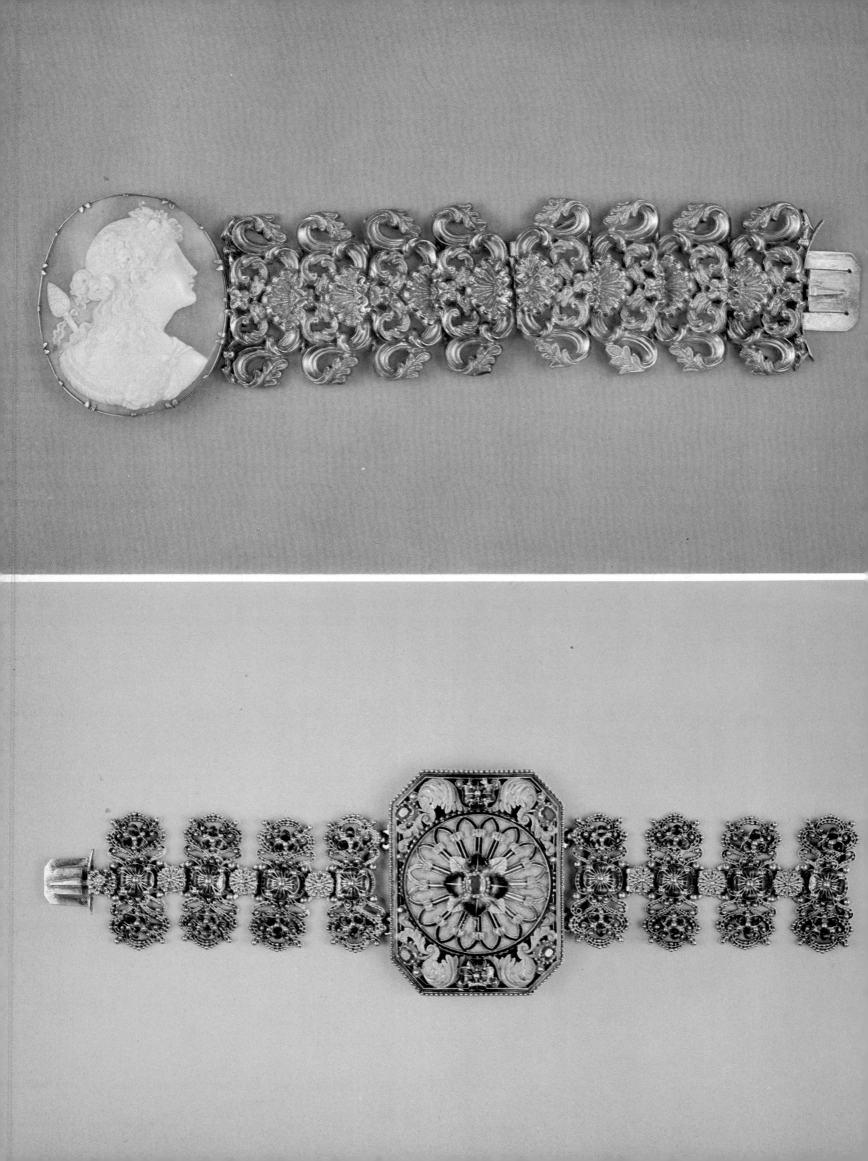

LEFT A stamped gold bracelet with a shell cameo of the French romantic period 1820–40. The girl depicted on the cameo is more decorative, less classical than the the cameos on page 42.

BELOW LEFT Here the eclecticism of 19th century taste is evident. The central piece of this gold bracelet, which is decorated with enamel, opens to reveal a miniature on ivory by Mansion dated 1832. The front of the miniature case is decorated with a pierced shape reminiscent of a gothic rose window, the flowers also have a gothic flavour, whilst the leafy scrolls have a more baroque look. The main feature of the small links is the granulation, typical of ancient Greek jewelry.

ABOVE RIGHT An English gothic bracelet, circa 1850 made of 15 carat gold, enamelled and set with rubies and emeralds. The enamelling and inscription in gothic writing are typical of English gothic work, following the pattern shown by N W Pugin in the Great Exhibition of 1851.

The 19th century gothic styles were expressed differently in France and England. In France, Froment-Meurice was the leading designer of gothic jewelry, and was much influenced by the sculpture found for example on the portals of French gothic cathedrals. RIGHT (see also page 4) A cast gold brooch of a women and a swan modelled by Wiese in Paris in the mid 1800s in the style of Froment-Meurice. ABOVE A more romantic sculptural piece by Rudolphi who was also working in Paris around the middle of the century.

Flowers and animals appear in different forms throughout the century, carved in jet and ivory, set with stones, enamelled, and made from seed pearls. Before 1860 animals represented were generally restricted to birds and serpents, but after 1860 other animals such as foxes, dogs and cats were also depicted, either enamelled or chased in gold or silver. A fashion for jeweled and enamelled insects in the 1860s reflects not only the taste for naturalism, but also the Victorian passion for novelties and curiosities.

The popularity of mourning jewelry continued in England, and was in even greater demand after the death of the Prince Consort when England adopted the Queen's practice of deep mourning. Whitby jet was carved into lockets, brooches, necklaces and earrings, whilst the French, having no native jet deposits produced a black glass substitute. Hair, traditionally associated with mourning was still arranged in patterns decorated with pearls and set under glass, or plaited and set in brooches or lockets. A new technique emerged of weaving necklaces, bracelets, earrings and pendants from hair, generally horse hair. Queen Victoria, whose importance as a fashion leader was minimal, did foster an interest in Scotland and Scottish tartans became fashionable all over Europe, whilst Scottish brooches enjoyed considerable popularity in England. The brooches were usually round plaid brooches set with Scottish agates, cairngorms, or copies of Celtic cloak pins.

RENAISSANCE REVIVAL

Renaissance pendants were copied and imitated in Italy, France and England from the 1840s. The outstanding exponent in England was Carlo Giuliano who came to England from Italy and settled in London. In France, Eugene Fontenay and Alphonse Fouquet were the leaders in this field.

LEFT An Italian revival pendant, adapted as a brooch. The subject of a sea monster, the use of a baroque pearl in the body of the creature, the emerald tail and the gold figure are all characteristic of Italian 16th century pendants. But the modelling of the figure is typically French 19th century, the diamonds are rose cut in grain settings, and there is no enamel.

BELOW LEFT A French pendant probably made by Alphonse Fouquet and enamelled by Beranger. The reverse is equally well made and finished, so the pendant can be worn either way round. It is quite easy to distinguish between renaissance revival work and the original pieces, because 19th century work has a more regular finish, the enamelling is better, the stones are of better quality and cut and they are in finer settings than were available during the 16th century.

RIGHT This magnificent chatelaine watch was made by Frederic Boucheron during the mid 19th century at the time of the lavish Second Empire. The piece is in the style of the French renaissance jewelry, with its winged mermaids and thick enamel; but a note of 19th century sentiment has crept in to the watch case cover. A cupid is depicted gazing at an hour glass below the inscription—"amour derobe les heures". An example of 19th century taste for novelty is also present— the wings of the mermaids are moveable.

FOLLOWING PAGE Another French renaissance revival piece, in which there is a classical lamp and pedestal which would not be found in anything made in the 16th century. Furthermore the enamel colours—the pinks and greens—are obviously a 19th century choice.

Classical Greco Roman jewelry was also copied and imitated in the 19th century. The Castellani family in Rome and later in London produced the finest classical reproductions.

ABOVE A pair of earrings and a pendant by Castellani, which bear the Castellani signature of two crossed 'C's. The earrings are not copies but classical goldsmithing techniques have been employed so that the use of unpolished gold and twisted wire contribute to the classical look. The pendant has a carved glass profile set with four claws, classical jewelry was always set with rub over settings.

RIGHT A mid 19th century French pendant decorated with enamel and granulation. With the exception of the enamel, the decorative motifs and techniques are reminiscent of classical forms but the size, the mixture of shapes (the triangle and semicircle linked with a rectangle) and the variety of surface decoration are all characteristics of mid 19th century design. The craftsmanship of this piece is superb, the back being as well finished as the front. It has been attributed to Fontenay on account of the white enamelled hanging ring, one of the characteristic marks of his work.

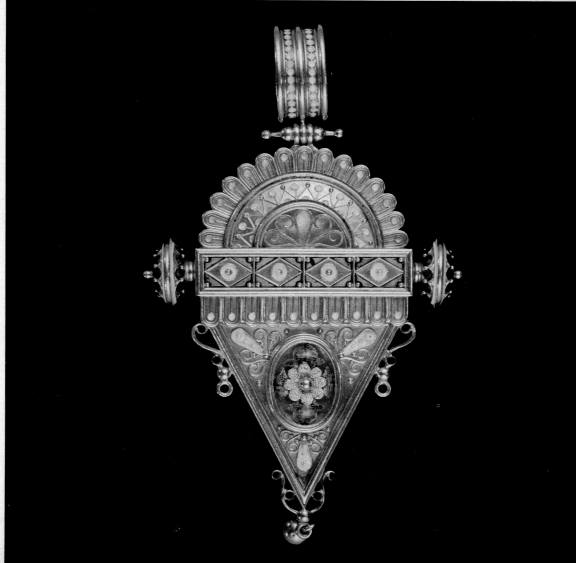

57

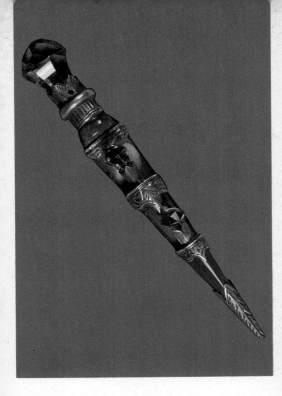

The Egyptian excavations initiated by the French in the early 19th century stimulated a vogue for Egyptian designs, the effect of which was seen in jewelry for some time.

LEFT A pair of enamel and gold scarab pins, one of which is set with a lapis, the other with an amethyst. The quality and colour of the enamel suggests French manufacture.
Above is a cruder scarab, set with rubies, sapphires, diamonds, turquoise, an emerald and a pearl. The pendant and chain display a mixture of Egyptian influence in the enamelled head and Victorian sentiment in the pearl-studded heart-shaped locket. In the locket is an enamelled scene suggesting an Egyptian landscape.

The Scottish cult encouraged by Queen Victoria's interest in Scotland and Balmoral illustrates the Victorian love of novelty. Plaid pins set with Scottish agates and cairngorms enjoyed immense popularity during the 1850s and '60s.

ABOVE AND RIGHT Two Scottish dirk pins circa 1850 set with moss agate, jasper, carnelian and cairngorms, a form of quartz native to Scotland.
FOLLOWING PAGE A celtic cloak pin in gold. These emanated from Ireland, and several were shown at the Great Exhibition of 1857 by West of Dublin. This one is a close imitation of a 7th century Irish Celtic cloak brooch but, as with most areas of Victorian design many pieces were based not just on one design but on several and ideas derived from different historical styles were mixed together.

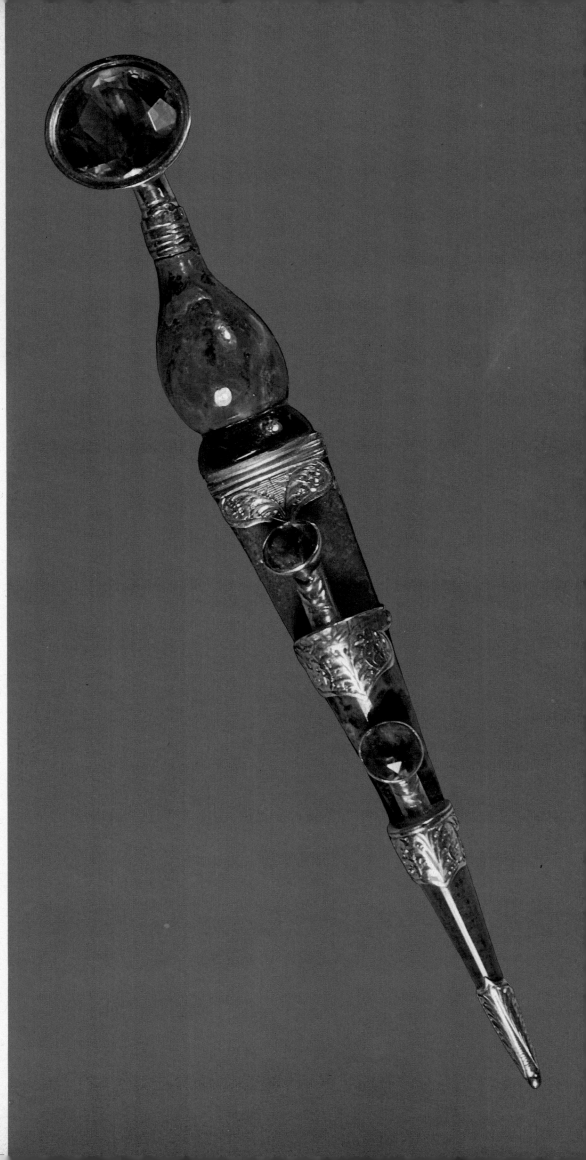

Another fashion stimulated by archeaology was that for Florentine and Roman mosaics, which developed particularly after the excavations of Herculaneum in the 1820s.

ABOVE AND BELOW LEFT Two brooches and a pendant of Florentine mosaic. *Left* An Italian peasant in traditional dress, a subject which appealed to the romantic taste of the 1820s–40s. *Above* A vase of flowers. *Below Left* The temple of Vesta in Rome. Roman ruins were another favourite subject for mosaic jewelry.

Whilst the jewelry of the beginning of the Victorian era is characterized by romanticism, delicacy, and the soft colours of pink and yellow topaz, the mid century was a period of flamboyant display, and the arrival of the Crinoline dictated huge conspicuous pieces of jewelry.

RIGHT An English bracelet circa 1860 set with a huge carbuncle or garnet cabochon into which diamonds are inlaid and flanked by two similar smaller carbuncles. Huge garnet cabochons and dark purple amethysts were immensely popular and often set into wide, cuff-like bracelets. This piece is particularly fine, the central garnet being of exceptional size and colour. FOLLOWING PAGE A gold bracelet, decorated with granulation and set with a variety of stones including chrysoprase, garnet, emerald, topaz, ruby and amethyst. It is also English made, earlier than the one on this page. The granulation and spacing gives the piece a light quality not often found in work of the 1860s. Although brilliant polychromy was a feature of mid Victorian work, the soft yellows and greens of topaz and chrysoprase suggest an earlier date, the late 1840s perhaps.

Other types of jewelry which are still quite easily obtainable include cameos, coral and carved larva. The popularity of cameos never ceased, but they changed little in style, so the only guide to dating cameos is by their settings. Coral, like shell cameos was carved in Southern Italy. Dark red and pale pink were the most popular shades, carved into flower and foliage sprays or birds, and worn by children or young women. The stick-like, natural forms of coral were also often used for necklaces or tiaras.

It was in the 19th century that for the first time individual jewelers and designers can be clearly distinguished and it is worth mentioning them. The architect of the House of Commons A.W.N. Pugin (1818–1852) did much to promote the taste for Gothic design, even in his designs for a set of jewelry which was shown at the Great Exhibition in 1851. Pugin looked to English Gothic ecclesiastical motifs for his ideas which were carved out in gold, enamel and cabochon stones. The French originator of the parallel French style was François Desirée Froment Meurice (1802–1853) a trained jeweler who took his ideas from French Gothic sculpture. Later he also produced enamelled jewels in the Renaissance style, and exhibited at the 1851 exhibition. The Castellani family are noted for their reproductions of classical Greek and Etruscan work. Fortunato Pio Castellani (1773–1865) opened a shop in Rome and produced extremely fine reproductions of classical jewelry. He discovered peasant jewelers in the marshes north of Rome who were still using antique methods which had changed very little since antiquity. His sons Augusto and Alessandro continued the business, making northern medieval-style pieces as well as the classical work. Much of the antique jewelry in the British Museum was acquired through Alessandro. Their work is marked with crossed cs. In England Robert Philips was a leading exponent of archaeological jewelry and received a decoration from the King of Naples for promoting coral jewelry in England. Philips had several Italian protégés, amongst whom was Carlo Giuliano who opened his own shop in Piccadilly. Giuliano is noted for his very fine enamel work which is exceptionally delicate. He produced many pieces based on archaeological and renaissance designs, from which he evolved his own style. Other leading jewelers were John Brogden, Eugene Fontenoy and Hunt and Roskell.

America, being a new country, produced very little jewelry till the late 19th century when Louis Comfort Tiffany became the outstanding American jewelry designer. His father Charles Tiffany had started making and selling jewelry in New York in 1848. In the '70s Tiffanys imported from Boucheron in Paris. At the turn of the century when the art nouveau style was at its height Tiffany exported to Samuel Bing in Paris for his shop 'Maison de L'Art Nouveau'.

THIS PAGE A variety of carved materials: ivory, coral, shell, jet and tortoiseshell. Coral was popular amongst the early Victorians until about 1865. It was thought suitable for children and young women. The favourite shade was dark red which was either carved, as in these pieces, or used in its natural branchlike state and incorporated in necklaces, tiaras and brooches. Most of the coral came from Naples. The English jeweler, Robert Philips of Cockspur Street, was decorated by the King of Naples for his contribution to the Neapolitan economy in popularizing coral in England. Shell carvings of one colour, such as the female head *above right* were set in jewelry as well as the bicoloured cameos. The fashions for ivory and jet developed later in the century. The main source was Whitby on the Yorkshire coast, where jet carving began around 1800. Later, mass production was introduced and, with the vogue for mourning after the death of the Prince Consort in 1861, jet was at the peak of popularity, carved with all the popular Victorian motifs; flowers, ivy leaves, geometric patterns and animals. When the mid Victorian taste for strong colour declined circa 1880, ivory came into its own. Dieppe was a major centre of ivory carving, three examples of which are shown *above*. Carved tortoiseshell was imported from the Orient towards the end of the century. RIGHT A parure of jet; a pair of earrings, brooch and locket all carved with flowers, and a necklace of jet acorns hanging from a jet chain.

LEFT Popular Victorian jewelry.
Left to Right:—a gold locket embossed with a typical Victorian pattern, a mixture of flowers, twisted wire and geometric design. A garnet bracelet with a machine stamped clasp. The oval gold locket is decorated with classical influenced granulation motif, framing a fine sentimental enamel miniature. The cameo is of lava, popular in late Victorian times. In the centre are two watch chain fobs, the one on the left is an engraved sard, the other a cornelian cameo. The tiger's claw whistle set in gold was a popular form of pendant after the British annexed India. This one is engraved as a gift and is dated May 1890. Italian mosaics were at their most popular during the early Victorian period but they were still produced in the late 19th century. The fine green cameo in a gold seed pearl frame probably dates from the first half of the century. At the bottom is a fine jet locket, set with stones and a silver figure; on the reverse side is a compartment for hair. The figure and gem set flowers suggest that it is French.

The United States was a new country in the 18th century and jewelry was not amongst the major considerations of its people. Silversmiths such as Revere and Richardson produced handsome functional pieces in the English style for the homes of the very wealthy, but very little jewelry. Such jewelry as was worn was mostly of European origin. American made jewelry was not only rare but also simple and in keeping with the austerity of the times.

CENTRE A 19th century 'sons of liberty' medallion. Due to its rarity, early American jewelry is much sought after.

FAR RIGHT Steel, gold and silver damascene locket. Damascene, (so called because it was widely practised in Damascus) is a technique of encrusting steel or iron with a more precious metal, in this case gold and silver. The design is oriental in flavour but this piece is probably late 19th century English made. Ivy leaves were a favourite Victorian motif.

Intricate seed pearl parures, linked with horse hair to a mother of pearl frame were plentiful during the late 18th and early 19th century. This taxing work declined during the 19th century but pearls were widely used for borders and were inlaid into other stones.

RIGHT A pair of long seed pearl earrings circa 1860.

Jewelers in many parts of Europe continued to use designs dating back to the 16th century. The origins of this piece are difficult to attribute but it may have come from Eastern Europe. There are elements of the Renaissance in the design, for example in the pendant pearls and in the alternate links reminiscent of Tudor roses and in the use of rubies and emeralds. But there is no enamelling and the delicate tracery of the piece is more suggestive of the 18th century, whilst the mixture of the two styles finally suggests the 19th century.

An exquisite enamelled necklace set with
rubies and peridots by Carlo Giuliano.

ABOVE An English brooch in the Indian style. Even before Queen Victoria became Empress of India, jewelry was designed in the East Indian style. John Brogden made the 15 carat 3-coloured gold frame which holds a panel of mother of pearl overlaid with green glass into which a scene in gold foil has been embedded. This technique is known as 'Indian Pitch' and is often found in antique Indian jewelry.

RIGHT A Brisson enamel bracelet. The chief features of Brisson enamel are its bright colours and the designs which include stars and circles often within a frame of more white circles. In the centre is either a semi-precious stone or a bright coloured piece of glass. The metal is generally silver but occasionally a piece enamelled on gold is found. Brisson enamelwork was done towards the end of the 19th century

LEFT This large enamelled cross is beautifully made and is equally magnificent front and back. It has no hallmarks but its boldness and colouring, coupled with the onion shaped terminals suggest Russian origins.

RIGHT A photograph of Lady Carew taken at the turn of the 20th century. She is dressed and bejewelled in the manner fashionable at the time; the quantity of the pieces and the size of the stones that she wears are characteristic of the opulent display favoured by wealthy Victorians and Edwardians. Her diamond choker, accompanied by two other necklaces was highly fashionable, whilst the several aigrettes placed in her hair probably date from an earlier period. The jewelry in this photograph is in complete contrast with the contemporary Art Nouveau shown in the next chapter.

69

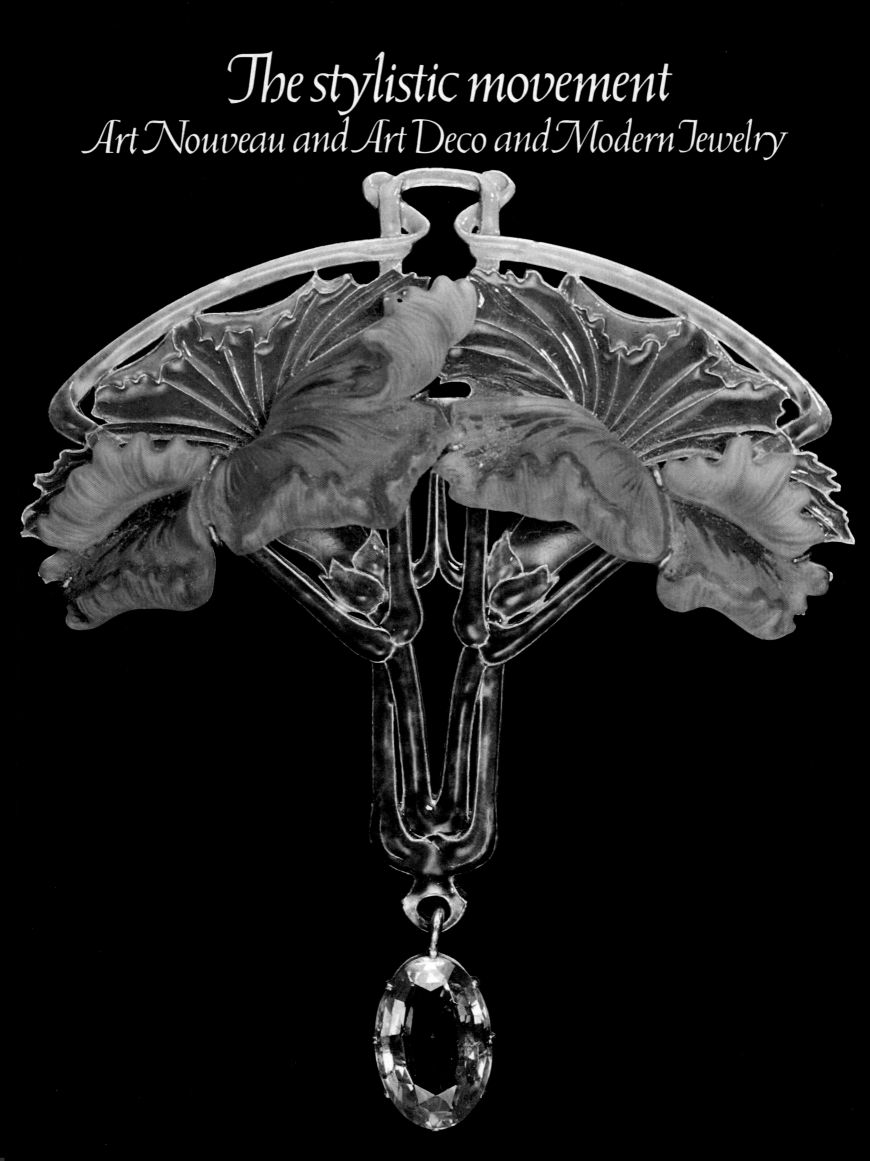

The stylistic movement
Art Nouveau and Art Deco and Modern Jewelry

In the last decade of the 19th century the flowing lines and sinister forms of Art Nouveau were expressed very effectively in jewelry.

LEFT Typical of the taste for exotic plants, this pendant shows a pair of succulent flowers. The misty mauve petals are constructed with polished *pliqué à jour* enamel and carved matt glass; the fluid outline is typical of the period. Suspended from this French piece is a faceted amethyst, which contrasts with the translucence of the carved glass.

The Art Nouveau style lasted only a short time, from the 1890s to the First World War, but it was a period of intense creativity, which affected all the applied arts. As we have already seen, 19th century design was generally derivative, the emphasis being on technical innovations, not new aesthetic ideas. The 19th century was a time of huge changes, social and economic; there were also movements afoot which were to culminate in the even greater changes of the 20th century, but in the meantime the wealthy and the powerful made every effort to maintain the status-quo. It was at the end of the century, in Paris, the hedonist centre of European fashion, that a style emerged which perhaps reflected a feeling of revolt against the repression and orthodoxy of the previous decades. Art Nouveau designers entirely rejected the classical vocabulary of decoration; replacing it with motifs derived from nature, and characterized by strong free flowing curves. Being a highly decorative style, it was supremely well suited to jewelry. The most outstanding pieces were made in Paris, and the most outstanding of the many designers working there was René Lalique.

Lalique took his ideas from the shapes and colours of exotic flowers such as orchids, irises and lilies, or from animals such as snakes and dragonflies, and in fact many of his pieces have a sinister quality. Another Art Nouveau feature often found is the head of a girl with a dreamy erotic expression, surrounded by swirling hair. He made a completely new departure in his use of materials which were rarely of high intrinsic value. Whilst establishment jewelers were using huge diamonds and pearls, Lalique used a combination of materials, horn, ivory, carved glass with enamel, and gemstones such as opals and moonstones. Eugene Feuillâtre, an assistant to Lalique, pioneered several new techniques in enamelling, whilst

pliqué à jour remained the most characteristic technique. Other noted French jewelers of the time were Georges Fouquet, Henri Vever and Lucien Gaillard. Since this jewelry does have a strong appeal it is much sought after and is expensive. It tends to be extremely delicate and many pieces must have been damaged and broken. Fortunately a large collection of work by Lalique is preserved in the Gulbenkian Museum in Lisbon. The jewelry of England, Scandinavia and Germany never reached such dizzy heights of imaginative design. In England the fashionable set was too conservative to enjoy the new style which was associated with decadence. So instead of the fashionable jewelers, it was the artist craftsmen such as C.R. Ashbee who explored the new ideas, and English Art Nouveau jewelry tends to have a somewhat amateur look. Silver, enamel, opals and pearls were the favourite materials. In Scandinavia, more professional work was produced, particularly in Denmark by George Jensen whose work is characterized by a sculptural use of silver, set with amber and cornelian. Similar work, although less bulbous and ebullient emerged from Germany and Vienna. The Germans mass produced small articles such as silver pendants, which can often be obtained today.

The years following the First World War witnessed the beginnings of a great change in jewelry styles. A war of unmatched horrors, a revolution in Russia, and the relentless crush of an urbanized technology created a sense of disillusionment which the intense gaiety of the jazz age twenties attempted to disguise. The interwar period is easily recognized by its painting, architecture, furniture and fabric designs. The strict lines of cubism replaced the foggy splendour of the post impressionists, and cubism in turn led to the precise geometric forms of

CONTINUED ON THE NEXT PAGE

PREVIOUS PAGE The mysterious face of a woman framed with flowing hair is a typical feature of Art Nouveau design. Three different examples of this are shown in these three French brooches. *Left* The brooch is of gold set with emeralds, suspended below it is a baroque pearl whose mishapen form particularly appealed to the Art Nouveau designer. *Right* A more dreamlike face carved in glass, in a characteristic curved frame of gold. *Below* The feeling of movement expressed in this style is well illustrated in the *pliqué à jour* gown which covers the form of a woman. It was the erotic qualities of Art Nouveau which contributed to the reputation for decadence sometimes still associated with it.

ABOVE LEFT A few American firms, such as L C Tiffany or Marcus and Company, were outstanding in creating Art Nouveau jewelry in the 1900s. J E Caldwell of Philadelphia also produced a limited amount. This opal, diamond and enamel necklace, although simpler and heavier in style than typical French work, has the same rich combination of enamel and opals, set in fluid curving frames. The work of Louis Comfort Tiffany in the early 20th century is renowned for its delicate designs and exquisite enamelling.

LEFT Two brooches and a pendant watch depicting snarling dragons. The dragons reflect an interest in the grotesque, and in fantasy, whilst the vitality of these pieces reflects the intensity of the style. The materials used, gold and precious stones are not typical of French Art Nouveau jewelry which was usually composed of a bigger variety of less valuable materials such as horn, glass or ivory.

The Art Nouveau style died with the first world war and was replaced in the twenties by the much brasher, bolder style of Art Deco. The soft, muted tones of Art Nouveau gave way to vibrant reds, yellows and greens, whilst geometric designs replaced the random organic curves of the previous era.

RIGHT This onyx, gold and pearl necklace is typical of the bold shapes and colour combinations of Art Deco designs. Circles, semicircles and crescents are a characteristic feature.

CONTINUED ON THE NEXT PAGE

Leger and Mondrian. In viewing the new forms of furniture and architectural design we see that the applied and decorative arts are intertwined as never before. Walter Gropius' Bauhaus group personifies this comprehensive approach to design. Although sadly few Bauhaus projects reached fruition, an important legacy was left, the influence of which is visible in most art of the interwar and postwar periods.

Art Deco is the name given to the styles of the '20s and '30s, derived from the *Exposition Internationale Des Arts Decoratifs* held in Paris in 1925. This exhibition set the tone of the period in placing all art forms on an equal footing, and the design of everything from electric appliances to skyscrapers was given the same aesthetic importance.

It does not take an expert eye to recognize Art Deco jewelry. Bright colour combinations which were absorbed from Leon Bakst's designs for the Ballets Russes and sharp, simplified geometric forms are certain indications of Art Deco. The dull red of coral is used with bright apple green jade, or deep blue lapis-lazuli. Black and white onyx and diamonds are used together with great effect. Bold colouring is not the only identifying characteristic of the period. Equally important are the concise well defined lines and strict geometric harmony, with straight lines and angles intersecting curves and circles. The two characteristic pieces of the thirties were the double clip and the huge cocktail ring. Both were made in a wide variety of materials from diamonds and precious stones to paste and base metal. It was during the '20s that platinum was introduced and used for the settings of

diamonds. And whilst Cartier, Van Cleef and Arpels, Lacloche and Tiffany were catering for the expensive end of the market, at the opposite end of the scale new plastics were being introduced and adopted for costume jewelry.

After the war, the strong somewhat stark outlines of Art Deco continued, and it was not till the late '50s that new styles began to emerge in jewelry. There was a new approach to the use of materials. Gold had previously been used either for setting, or decoration polished, engraved or for filigree. Jewelers such as Andrew Grima or Gilbert Albert cast gold into natural forms, such as tree bark, or shells, achieving completely new textures and forms in the metal. Similarly, stones which had always been cut or polished in some way since their earliest use, were used in their crystal form. These were moves towards more random shapes and textures, away from the clearly defined, ordered look of Art Deco work. Since the early '60s an ever increasing number of designers, and craftsmen jewelers have emerged, producing a wide variety of designs in a wide variety of materials. There are the architectural designers whose work is simple and clean cut, the pop designers, the sculptural designers who make tiny sculptures, and those who use engineering components, screws and cogs. There are those who use diamonds and those who use polymer resins. The large established firms such as Van Cleef and Arpels or Bul, continue to supply the most costly pieces to the richest clients, but their designs remain traditional and subservient to the magnificent stones used. Instead it is from the numerous designers in America, Europe and Japan that the most interesting and varied designs come.

CONTINUED FROM PREVIOUS PAGE This
piece is made of natural materials, but
similar pieces were mass produced in the
new plastics being introduced all the time.
At the other end of the scale, the traditional gemstones enjoyed considerable
popularity. LEFT A pair of beautifully
made diamond and ruby earrings illustrate the straight lined geometry also
found in cinema architecture of the '20s
and '30s. *Below* the most common item of
jewelry between the wars: a double clip,
either worn as one brooch, or as two
separate clips. Here rubies, emeralds and
sapphires form an exuberant colour
combination.

ABOVE A delightful brooch of three
columns and a palm tree set with baquette
diamonds, emeralds and rubies. This
piece, dated 1928, is evocative of the
life style in the south of France in the '20s
and '30s, as depicted by Scott Fitzgerald
and Evelyn Waugh for example.

Cartier was at a peak of popularity
during this period, and much of the
Cartier work included oriental curved
stones, particularly carved jade, often
combined with coral. Coral and onyx
was another popular colour
combination. ABOVE RIGHT A modest
brooch by Cartier of gold, onyx,
diamond and turquoise enamel shows
something of the striking colours
fashionable at the time.

During the years of recovery after the second world war, it took some time for any strong creative impetus to be discernible in jewelry design. But in the late '50s, designer craftsmen with new ideas began to emerge in Europe, America and Japan. In the last 15 years the field of jewelry design has become so wide and varied that only a suggestion of what is happening can be given here.

ABOVE RIGHT A natural crystal set in gold with diamonds by Andrew Grima, one of the leading modern jewelers of the world. The gold setting has an organic texture which harmonizes with the natural form of the crystal. This mixture of materials in their original form combined with gold cast into random textures and shapes is characteristic of contemporary jewelry in the 1960s and '70s.

RIGHT A set of aquamarine and diamond pieces by Charles de Temple, including earrings, bracelet, ring and brooch. The irregular forms of the gold setting and the contrast between the rough textured gold and the perfectly cut aquamarines is a recent innovation in jewelry design.

75

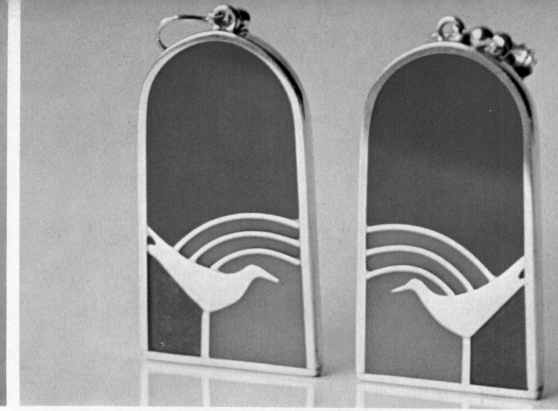

ABOVE A gold and cabochon tourmaline ring by the authoress. Set with tiny tubes of gold it illustrates a fashion in contemporary jewelry for making a setting with repeated units such as circles, squares or rods.

LEFT A collection of jewelry by Wendy Ramshaw. There is a pendant, four ring sets of gold set with different coloured chalcedony and agates, and a single ring. The single ring is turned on a lathe, a completely new technique in jewelry, whilst the ring sets are composed of individual rings which may be assembled in different orders achieving a different pattern each time. The designer supplies the perspex stands with her rings in order that they may be displayed like sculpture when not being worn.

ABOVE RIGHT A pair of silver and coloured resin earrings by Susanna Heron. These show the use of a new material, plastic resin in rich transparent colours. They also show a new pictorial approach to jewelry design.

Naturalism and the use of intrinsically valueless materials with gold and diamonds has again been adopted. Since the Art Nouveau period, most jewelry was either composed entirely of valuable stones and gold or of valueless materials. RIGHT A gold flower pendant by Roger Doyle set with diamonds and ivory shows both these features. Also its delicacy in comparison with the aggressive quality of the aquamarine set reflects the variety in jewelry design today.

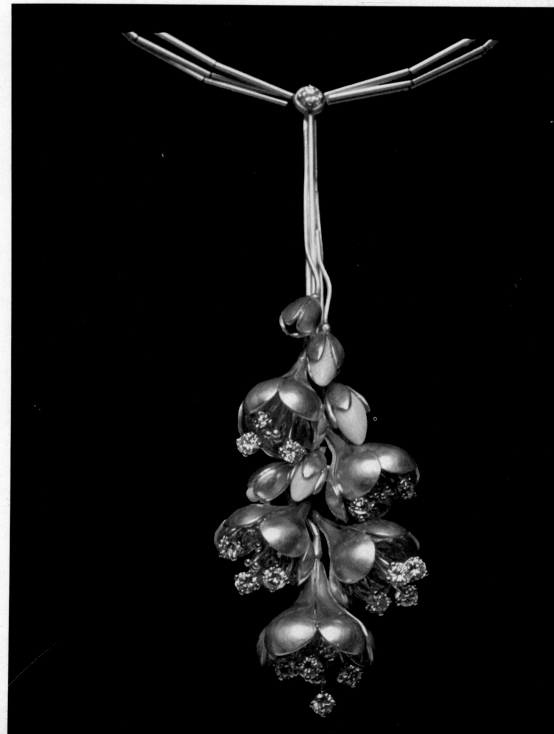

77

Eastern work through the ages

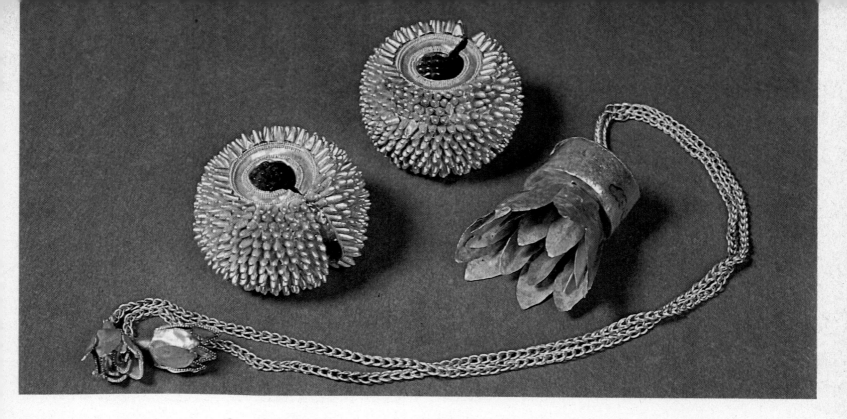

The only common feature of the jewelry described in this chapter is that it is all non-European. Chinese, Tibetan, Indian, African and pre-Columbian pieces have been included, so there is only room here for a brief outline of the jewelry produced in each country.

INDIA

India has huge natural resources of precious and semi-precious stones as well as deposits of gold and silver, so it is not surprising that some of the earliest highly coloured and imaginative jewelry was produced by that creative nation. Ancient sculptures testify that Indian jewelry, in common with most South Asian jewelry, has always tended to consist of ostentatious but brilliantly detailed metalwork, whilst archeology has shown that the use of rich colour in stones and enamel has long been an outstanding feature. The profusion of forms:- earrings, bracelets, belts, anklets, armlets, hair ornaments, turban ornaments and rings shows that the Indians loved decorating their entire bodies with jewels.

The Muslim invasions of the 16th Century introduced Persian techniques of enamelling and stone setting to India. It is perhaps the Moghul style jewelry which is the most splendid ever produced in India. Mina enamel, the cloisonné enamel work brought by the moghuls is still famed for its colour and designs but the quality and colours of 17th and 18th century enamel in necklaces, pendants, bracelets and turban ornaments is unparalleled. Flowers, birds, and animals are the chief decorative motifs; pearls, emeralds, rubies and diamonds were combined with the enamelled links. The method of inlaying jade with gold, which in turn held precious stones was also a Moghul introduction used not only for jewelry but for sword handles, bowls and vases too.

CHINA

Although China has an ancient artistic tradition which includes highly skilled metal working, the conception of decorative or valuable ornaments for self adornment has never greatly appealed to the Chinese. From the T'ang dynasty (618–906) A.D., the Chinese system of three grades of society: the military, the civil servants and the peasants was strengthened by compulsory annual civil service examinations. Chief amongst them were painting, calligraphy and poetry which reinforced the Chinese propensity for perpetuating traditional styles. During the S'ung dynasty (960–1279) more jewelry was produced, but styles changed little after the late S'ung period. Head ornaments, ranging from tiaras to hairpins were the most important forms of jewelry. The materials used were not of any importance for their intrinsic value and include bamboo, wood and ivory. Coral was assumed to have magical properties but a more important aspect of the significance attached to materials was that of status. Each grade in the civil service was expressed by a button of, for example, rose, quartz or silver, placed at the top of the conical headress worn by every Mandarin. The most striking feature, unique to Chinese jewelry, is the use of the iridescent blue feathers from the breast of a tiny oriental Kingfisher. The feathers were mounted in gold or silver, with finely carved jade, coral, pearls, amber and filigree. (Opposite—see following page.)

Jade is the other material chiefly associated with China but it was not used to any large extent in jewelry. Powerful Mandarins wore long necklaces of carved or plain jade beads and carved jade beads and armlets were stitched onto clothes.

TIBET

Tibetans are very different from their neighbours, the Chinese and the Indians. The monastery was the focal point of Tibetan life, the centre of trade, culture and social life. Much of their jewelry is devotional. Turquoise is the most characteristic feature of Tibetan jewelry, often accompanied by coral and pearls.

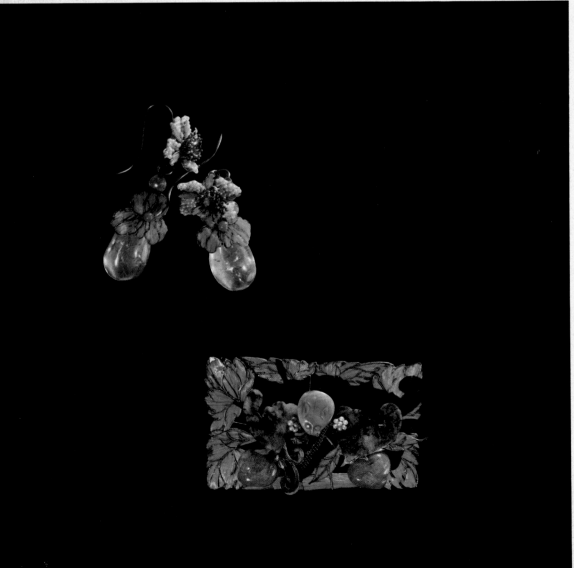

PREVIOUS PAGE LEFT A detail of hair pin of the early Ch'ing dynasty (1644–1912). The hairpin is of silver with kingfisher feather inlay and represents the water dragon. It is made up of 13 different sections hinged together, enabling the dragon to flap its fins and tail. The waterdragon usually represents the emperor, it also is a feminine symbol. In this case, it is recognized because of the absence of legs and the exaggeration of the fins and tail.

PREVIOUS PAGE Some very early examples of Indian jewelry found in a burial chamber at Souttoukeny, South India: a pair of earrings and a pendant on a fine, unsoldered chain. The pendant represents a lotus flower, an image which constantly appears in all Indian art, and symbolizes fertility in the Buddist religion. Very little early Indian jewelry has survived but these pieces testify to the expertise of Indian goldsmiths at the time.

LEFT A Chinese pendant and earrings set with kingfisher feathers and rock crystal, dating from the 18th century.

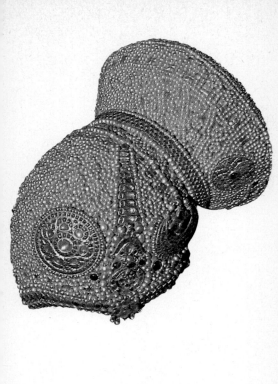

ABOVE LEFT Although most Chinese jewelry had the function of indicating the wearer's rank or status, this bracelet appears to have been made for purely decorative purposes. It is a gold bracelet of the Ming dynasty (1368–1644), decorated with dragon's head terminals and filigree, and inlaid with stones, possibly agate. The heads and the designs in the filigree are all of symbolic importance. The craftsmanship is superb, the bracelet is hinged in the centre back, whilst the dragons' heads slot together with a connecting tongue.

ABOVE A beautiful 17th century headdress for a female deity from a South Indian temple. It is covered with pearls applied in rich patterns, and set with rubies, diamonds and emeralds in gold. The Iranian influence on Indian culture through the Moghuls was enormous.

RIGHT A portrait of Abdulhamid I, Sultan of Turkey 1774–89. The taste for luxurious self adornment and surroundings which the Moslem rulers took to India is shown here. The front of his clothes is encrusted with gems and in his headdress is a huge ornament very similar to the turban jewels of India.

81

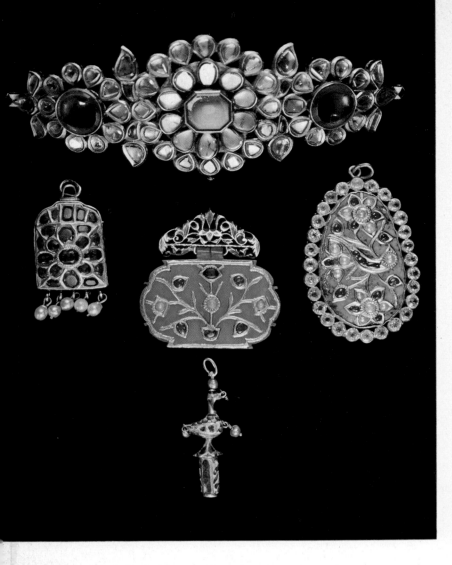

WEST AFRICA

Although the Egyptians were using gold more than 2,000 years before Christ, the use of gold in the rest of the African continent is comparatively recent. The gold desposits in West Africa on the river Niger have probably only been exploited since the 10th century. The Ashanti, centred round the Niger delta had the reputation of being one of the most warlike tribes in Africa, and this martial energy was matched by an astonishing creative and artistic ability, displayed particularly by the goldsmiths. Their virtuosity in lost wax casting was outstanding, as was their instinct for pattern in their beaten gold work. It is probable that their designs were mainly symbolic. Kings and princes wore gold rings on every finger and toe, as well as anklets, necklets, and pectorals; for ceremonial occasions they were accompanied by retainers wearing 'soul-bearing' badges, patterned roundels, as additional expressions of the wealth and power of the ruler. In the 19th century the Ashanti empire was crushed by the British. Thousands of Ashanti artifacts were lost or destroyed.

PRE COLUMBIAN GOLD

The gold of South America was famous, even in the 16th century when the Spanish conquistador Pizarro with 200 men made the perilous voyage to the South American continent in search of El Dorado, the legendary city. Instead, they found and destroyed the Inca civilization in Peru together with most of the gold work.

In the religions of all the pre-Columbian nations, the Incas, the Aztecs and the Maya, the sun was of paramount importance. Like the Egyptians many centuries earlier, they regarded gold as an earthly manifestation of the sun. As in most primitive cultures, their art was symbolic and functional, though little is known of the exact significance of their designs. What is clear from the goldwork which survived the melting pot, is that almost all the techniques known today were practised by the American Indians. They were highly skilled in the art of *cire perdue* casting, an extravagent method which reflects the abundance of gold available to the goldsmiths. Pieces of jewelry for decorating every part of the body were produced, huge pectorals, nose ornaments, earrings, headdresses, pendants, necklets, armlets and anklets of beads. Besides jewelry, gold ceremonial sculptures and implements were made for the temples and to accompany the dead. The designs are chiefly stylized animals and geometric patterns. The animals, amongst them eagles, crocodiles and frogs, probably represented spirits.

The quantity and importance of gold in pre-Columbian art is clear. 6,700 pieces of sculpture and jewelry are preserved in the Bogota Museum of Gold despite the indiscriminate destruction till this century. But the Incas did embellish their goldwork with coloured stones, emeralds, turquoise, lapis-lazuli and rock crystal, whilst the Aztecs in Mexico utilized the natural resources of turquoise for theirs.

RIGHT A Tibetan necklace of gold set with turquoise.

FAR LEFT A collection of Indian jewelry made between the 17th and 19th centuries shows Moghul influence.
Top A headband set with foiled rubies and rough cut diamonds. The recessed setting edge is typical of Indian work. The reverse is enamelled with small buds and floral designs. *Left* The ruby-set pendant is early 18th century and from it hang many pearls, another typical feature of Indian jewelry. *Centre* A pendant of mutton fat jade set with pearls, rubies and sapphires, made in Delhi in the 17th century. These pendants were worn for protection against palpitations of the heart. *Right* A turquoise, pearl and ruby pendant framed with diamonds. The design of flowers and a bird is characteristic. *Below* An enamelled bird pendant, probably 18th century. All the gold in these pieces is 22 carat.

LEFT A 19th century enamelled necklace, which shows something of the colourful richness of Indian work. Both sides of the links are enamelled and this piece is unusual in having an enamelled clasp. Indian necklaces are generally fastened with a cord bound with gold thread. From the central pendant hangs a large emerald.

RIGHT A selection of 19th century Chinese jewelry made for the export market. In the late 19th century there was a vogue for Chinoiserie in England. The carved stone brooch *top* depicts five old men at a ceremony, and the dragon is in 22 carat gold signed with a Chinese character. The enamel brooch *left* is of European Chinoiserie design and the peacock blue and crimson are typical of Chinese work. The carved lacquer panel is set in silver. Carved lacquer was imported to Europe from the 17th century and incorporated in furniture by English cabinet makers. The use of lacquer in jewelry, however, was a 19th century development. The fine jade bracelet shows something of the colour variations in the stone, and the silver bracelet has dragon's head terminals and is decorated with champleré enamel. Bracelets with two animal head terminals have been produced all over the world in separate cultures, for example, by the Greeks and by the Persians.

83

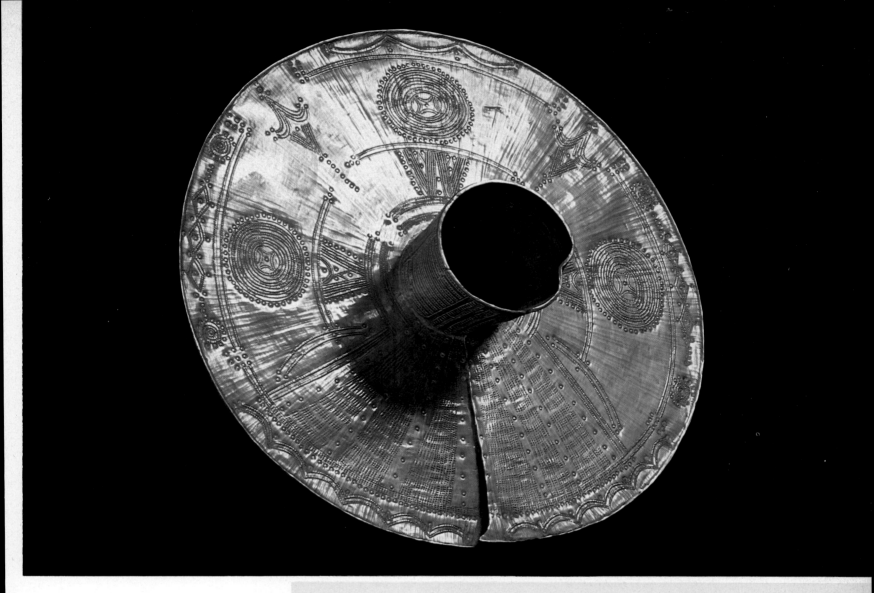

ABOVE An Ashante anklet from Nigeria. The craftsmanship in this piece is outstanding, and its bold conception is striking. It has been beaten into a circle and the whole surface decorated with an imaginative variety of stamped designs.

RIGHT A gold mask pendant from Peru. The exact purpose of this pendant mask is open to speculation. Several gold funerary masks have been discovered but their symbolic significance is unknown. The significance of the knife LEFT is also unknown. It is a ceremonial knife surmounted by a hollow dumpy figure who must represent a ruler or a diety. In his ears he appears to have a pair of ear scoops, cylindrical ornaments which were inserted in the ear lobes. Despite the sophistication of the Inca and Aztec civilizations that the Spaniards found in the 16th century, neither civilization had existed for much more than 200 years, so these pieces are of the 15th or 16th centuries.

Gemstones and metals

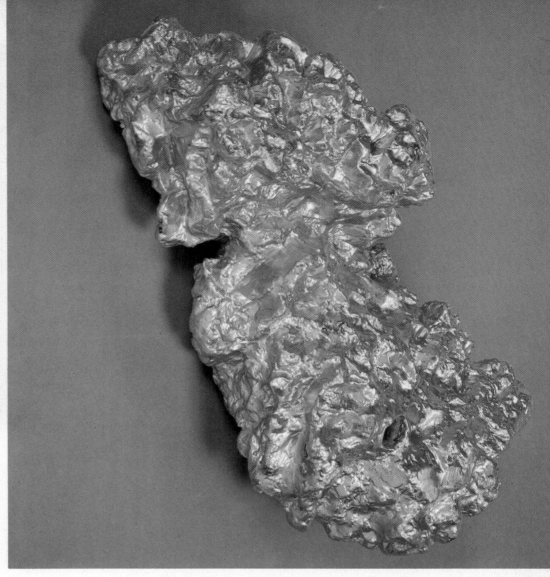

LEFT A selection of cut gemstones (see page 90).

METALS

Gold

The most malleable, ductile and durable of metals. It does not tarnish. Its ductility allows it to be beaten to fine leaf or drawn to very fine wire without breaking. It is alloyed with other metals to obtain a variety of colours. The proportion of gold in an alloy is measured in carats, pure gold being assessed at 24 parts.

Silver

Shares many of the properties of gold. It is softer and more brittle than gold and it tarnishes. Standard silver has 925 parts of pure silver with 75 parts of alloy to the 1,000.

Electrum

A natural alloy of gold and silver, thought by the Greeks to be a separate metal.

Platinum

A hard, ductile and untarnishable metal used particularly for mounting diamonds. It has a high melting point (1,755°C) and is, therefore, employed where heat-resistance is required. It was first discovered in the early 19th century but its hardness made it difficult to work

so it was not generally used till the late 19th century. It was particularly popular in the 1920s and 30s.

Pinchbeck

An alloy of copper and zinc used to simulate gold. It was invented by the watchmaker, Christopher Pinchbeck, in the early 18th century.

Cut Steel

Faceted and polished steel resembling cut stones. It was first produced in Woodstock, mass produced by Matthew Boulton in the late 18th century, first in Soho, later in Birmingham.

Berlin Iron

Finely cast iron jewelry originally made as a side line at the Prussian Royal Iron Foundry in Berlin. Popular during the early 19th century.

ABOVE LEFT Australian gold in calcite. Mined gold is generally found in quartz which has the same crystaline structure as calcite. The Egyptians were the earliest gold miners. To obtain the gold, the ore-bearing quartz is crushed finely and washed. The quartz being lighter is

washed away leaving the heavier gold which is then melted.

ABOVE The Welcome Nugget found in Bakery Hill, in Ballarat, Victoria, Australia on 11th June 1858. Its weight is 2,217 oz, 16 dwt (troy weight). (Troy weight: the weight used by jeweler for precious metals. There are 20 dwt (penny weights) to the ounce). Gold is obtained in two ways; either in nugget form in river beds from alluvial sources, or by mining. It is supposed that gold was first discovered in the 6th millenium BC from alluvial deposits. It is found all over the world and every race with the exception of the New Zealand Maori has showed an interest for it. The chief sources today are South Africa, Australia and Russia.

FOLLOWING PAGE A fibrous mass of native silver. Many of the properties of gold are shared by silver and it is often found in association with gold. It is seldom found in its pure state but in natural alloy with other metals. The natural alloy of gold and silver is known as electrum. It was liked and used by the Greeks who thought it was a separate metal.

CENTRE Two emerald crystals and a selection of cut stones. *Left* Emerald crystals as they are found. *Right* A group of Chatham synthetic emerald crystals. These crystals are made by a process introduced by the American C F Chatham. *Front* Four facetted emeralds.

Flawless emeralds are extremely rare and most stones are marred by flaws and inclusions which greatly reduce their transparency. Emerald owes its beauty almost entirely to its colour and does not display the same sparkle and brilliance of some other gemstones. As a consequence of this, and also due to the extremely brittle nature of the stone, it is seldom cut in styles employing many small facets. The stones are generally cut in rectangular or octagonal shapes. (rectangles with the corners cut off). The earliest known source of emeralds was a group of mines by the Red Sea in Egypt. Due to the poor colour and the flawed nature of the stones found there mining is no longer profitable and South America is now the most important source of emeralds the stones are also mined in both Colombia and Brazil. The Colombian mines are very ancient and have produced some of the finest emeralds in the world. Another source which produces very fine quality stones, marketed under the name Sandawana emeralds, was discovered in Rhodesia in 1956. Owing to the flawed nature of the Sandawana crystals cut stones of over a quarter of a carat in weight are rare.

LEFT A diamond crystal in kimberlite and a brilliant cut diamond. The vast majority of diamonds occur in a basic igneous rock called kimberlite. It is in this rock that diamonds occur in Africa and Russia and it is assumed that all other deposits of diamond (alluvial deposits) had their origin in such rocks, being transported to their present position by rivers. The most usual shape in which diamond crystals are found is the octahedron which consists of eight triangular faces. This shape lends itself very well to being cut in half, just above the centre, and faceted into two brilliant cut stones. The brilliant cut was especially adapted for diamonds so that, in a well-cut stone, all the light entering the top of the stone would be refracted and reflected round the back facets and

88

returned to the eye, thus displaying the well known brilliance of diamonds.

Diamond is composed of pure carbon and so is graphite. It is the difference in crystal structure between the two which causes the vast difference in properties. Diamond is the hardest natural substance known whilst graphite is one of the softest. The majority of diamonds found display faint shades of colour in an essentially colourless stone, although the best quality diamonds are completely colourless. Deeper shades of yellow, brown and green also occur as do pink, deep blue and deep green though the latter colours are extremely rare.

The earliest sources of diamond were in India and these mines produced many of the large historically famous diamonds including the Koh-i-Noor and the deep blue Hope diamond. Diamonds were discovered in Brazil, near Rio de Janeiro in 1725 and in South Africa in 1867. Many areas in South Africa produce diamonds and it is now the most important source of gem quality diamonds.

BELOW LEFT A selection of Beryls showing the variety of types and colours. Sea green emeralds; blue and violet acquamarines; yellow or golden heliodor; pink morganite; and colourless goshenite. The main sources of aquamarine are Brazil, Ceylon and the Ural Mountains.
BELOW RIGHT Corundum, which is the family name for a group of stones including ruby and sapphire, occurs in several different colours. Pure corundum is colourless but natural colourless material of gem quality is seldom cut. The 'white sapphire' used frequently in jewelry is almost always synthetic. Ruby occurs in a fine blood red and pinkish, purplish and brownish shades of red. 'Pigeon blood' is the name sometimes applied to the best coloured stones. Sapphire varies from a fine cornflower blue through paler blues and a blackish or greenish blue which is less valuable. Other colours of corundum include pink, yellow, green, orange and purple. These colours are known as fancy sapphires and are generally named sapphire with a colour prefix, eg. green sapphire.

The finest rubies, though generally rather small stones, are found in Burma and are a pinkish red colour. Rubies from Thailand, another important source, are often spoilt by shades of brown and purple in their colour. Ceylonese rubies are usually pale pink in colour and can often be called pink sapphires. There is no sharp division between rubies and pink sapphires, since the difference lies solely in colour.

The name Kashmir is often synonymous with the finest sapphires though the output from this source is very small. The main sources of good quality sapphires are Thailand and Burma, other sources include Ceylon, USA and Australia. The Australian sources produce very large quantities of stone generally of a dark blue, blackish or greenish colour. Ceylon is the source of most of the fancy coloured corundums.

Corundum is second in hardness to diamond and since it is not generally brittle the stones of this group are eminently suitable for jewelry.

ABOVE A variety of gemstones displaying different styles of cutting. These two pictures show most of the colour varieties of beryl, zircon and tourmaline (see key).

The beryl family includes not only emerald and aquamarine but yellow beryl (also called heliodor), golden beryl, colourless beryl (called white beryl or achroite) and pink beryl (also called morganite).

Zircon occurs in many different colours, among them red, yellow, green and brown. The usual colours seen in jewelry are blue and white but these are the result of heat-treating red brown stones and these colours do not occur naturally.
The main sources of zircon are Ceylon, Indo-China and Thailand.

Tourmaline surpasses almost all other gemstones in its range of colours. The best known colours are pink and green but other colours are red, yellow, honey yellow, blue, dark blue, white, brown, black and purple. Tourmaline also produces unusual bi-coloured and tri-coloured stones, one of which is illustrated ABOVE LEFT TOP CENTRE. At one time different names were applied to each colour but today they are all called tourmaline with the colour prefix, eg pink tourmaline.

A large peridot (called olivine by mineralogists) is also illustrated ABOVE LEFT and shows the characteristic yellow green colour of this gemstone. ABOVE RIGHT illustrates two varieties of opal, the bright red fire opal found in Mexico and the black opal which is the most valuable variety of opal.

Several examples of red and pink spinel are also illustrated. This stone has often been confused with ruby and several famous 'rubies' have transpired to be red spinels. Among these is the Black Prince's 'ruby'.

RIGHT A selection of topazes. Topaz occurs in several different colours including colourless, pink, yellow and blue. The majority of topaz found is colourless and is called white topaz.
The next most abundant colours of topaz are the blue and green blue stones, which are similar to aquamarine.
The colours most frequently seen in jewelry are the shades of yellow to

Above left

1 Fluorite
2 Zircon
3 Tourmaline
4 Tourmaline
5 Garnet (Hessonite)
6 Garnet (Denantoid)
7 Phenakite
8 Olivine (Peridot)
9 Zircon
10 Sphene
11 Garnet (Spessartine)
12 Corundum (Yellow Sapphire)
13 Quartz (Amethyst)
14 Beryl (Heliodor)
15 Spodumene (Kumzite)
16 Beryl (Aquamarine)
17 Quartz (Rock Crystal)
18 Chrysoberyl
19 Zircon
20 Zircon
21 Sphalerite
22 Tourmaline
23 Apatite
24 Amblygonite
25 Spinel
26 Scapolite
27 Andalusite
28 Zircon
29 Fluorite
30 Chrysoberyl
31 Sillimanite (Fibrolite)
32 Tourmaline
33 Zircon

Above

1 Topaz
2 Brazilianite
3 Opal
4 Scheelite
5 Danburite
6 Beryl (Emerald)
7 Fire Opal
8 Beryl
9 Garnet (Almandine)
10 Cordierite (Lolite)
11 Topaz
12 Corundum (Purple Sapphire)
13 Labradorite
14 Apatite
15 Tourmaline
16 Beryl (Morganite)
17 Topaz
18 Quartz (Citrine)
19 Moon stone
20 Spinel
21 Garnet (Pyrope)
22 Fluorite
23 Garnet (Hessonite)
24 Sinhalite
25 Spinel
26 Black opal
27 Tourmaline
28 Diopside
29 Topaz
30 Beryl
31 Danburite
32 Tourmaline
33 Orthoclase

sherry brown and the pink stones. Both red and pink topaz are extremely rare in nature and the vast majority of the pink topaz on the market is the result of heat-treatment of suitable sherry coloured crystals.

Much confusion still exists between topaz and the two varieties of quartz, citrine (yellow) and cairngorm (brown). It is sometimes difficult for the untrained person to distinguish between citrine and topaz by eye alone, but each stone has a characteristic which is helpful. Firstly topaz is a much brighter stone than quartz. This is due, in part, to the fact that topaz is harder and consequently takes a better polish. Secondly quartz is frequently uneven in colour whereas the topaz is much more likely to be even.

Some of the yellow coloured topazes are said to fade on long exposure to bright sunlight. Topaz suffers from the disadvantage of being very easily broken. Owing to the long thin shape of the original crystal most stones are cut in long thin shapes which are very easily broken. The main source of the yellow to sherry yellow colours is Brazil while many of the fine blue stones originate in Russia.

BELOW RIGHT A selection of cabochon cut starred and cat's-eye stones.

Asterism (star stones) and chatoyancy (cat's-eyes) are both caused by numerous thread-like inclusions in the stones. Cat's-eyes contain fine fibres or fibrous cavities running parallel through the crystal in one direction only. When the stone is cut en cabochon (with a domed top) the fibrous inclusions reflect light at right angles to their direction. It is simplest to compare this effect to a reel of cotton which, if held under a light, produces a bright streak of light up the length of the cotton reel.

In star stones the fibrous inclusions run in either two or three directions. The number of possible directions of threads is dictated by the crystal structure of the stone. The stones have to be cut en cabochon to display these optical effects. Chatoyancy occurs frequently in chrysoberyl and quartz and more rarely in tourmaline and beryl.

Asterism is shown most frequently by ruby and sapphire and sometimes by rose quartz, green zircon and aquamarine. Almandine garnets and spinel occasionally show four rayed stars.

FOLLOWING PAGES BELOW Azurite and malachite which have formed in conjunction. Malachite is often found together with azurite; when the pieces are cut and polished a blue and green banded stone is produced. Malachite is dark green and banded while azurite is named for its typical azure blue colour. Both these stones are very soft but this does not appear to limit their use in jewelry. Malachite, particularly, is extensively used both for jewelry and ornamental purposes, such as inlay work.

FOLLOWING PAGE RIGHT A selection of the chalcedony varieties of quartz. There are two types of quartz called crystalline quartz and chalcedony or cryptocrystalline quartz. Cryptocrystalline means that the stones are composed of masses of submicroscopic crystals. Crystalline quartz includes several well known gemstones such as amethyst, citrine,

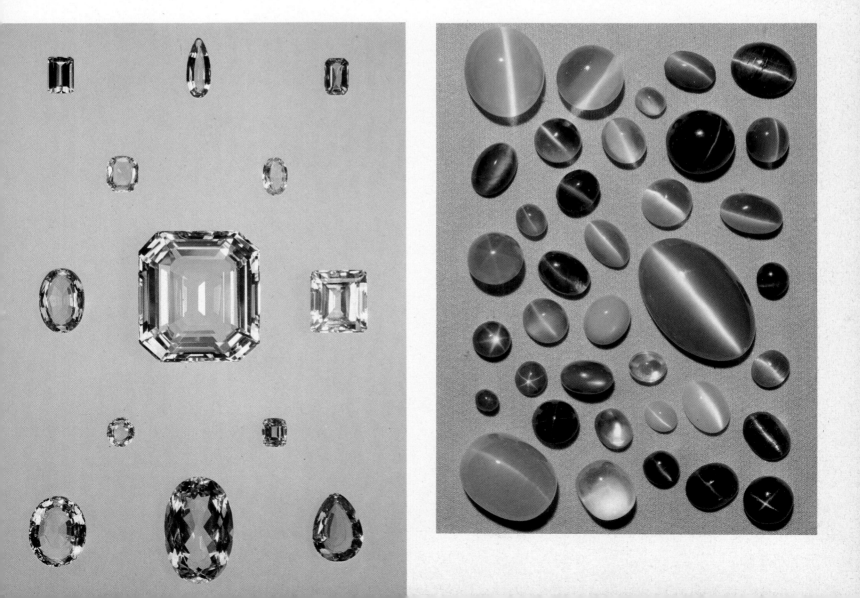

RIGHT *cont* smokey quartz and rose quartz, The varieties of chalcedony are numerous and include plasma, bloodstone, chrysoprase, cornelian, sard, onyx and all the different types of agate. The picture RIGHT illustrates:
Centre Two types of moss agate, so named because of the inclusions of other minerals which assume tree-like forms.
Right Banded agate
Below left Colourless chalcedony in its natural state and a ring of banded agate
Centre A necklace of cornelian beads and a handle of apple green chrysoprase, its characteristic colour.
Right A cameo of carved plasma.

ABOVE A variety of different types of garnets including crystals and cut stones. Garnet is the name applied to a group of gemstones but only the red varieties have been frequently used in jewelry.
The many different types include:
Grossular garnet—an opaque green stone occurring in South Africa
Hessonite garnet—an orange red to honey yellow

Pyrope garnet—a fine deep crimson red much used in Victorian rose cut garnet jewelry
Almandine garnet—a medium to deep red generally with a purplish tinge
Spessartite garnet—a rare reddish orange or yellow variety
Demantoid garnet—a bright green variety. The very fine green stones, found mainly in Russia, are now rare.

TECHNICAL TERMS:

Annealing
Softening metal by heating it to make it malleable.
Assay
The testing of metals to ensure that they are of a standard fineness.
Box Setting
A box like closed setting the sides of which are pressed over the stone to hold it in place.
Cameo
A carved gem or shell, in which the carved design stands out against a background of a different colour.
Cannetille
A partially mass production process of decorating matt finished stamped gold units with rather course filigree, popular during the 19th century.
Champlevé
A method of enamelling, when recesses are carved from the metal and filled with enamel. A line of metal is left between the carved out areas.
Chasing
The method of decorating a metal surface using punches and a hammer. There are two types of chasing: flat or with repoussé. Flat chasing decorates the front of a flat piece of metal without cutting away any metal. Repoussé chasing is applied to the front surface of a piece of metal to bring out the detail of a raised pattern beaten or embossed from the back.

Cire Perdue

The method of casting an object in metal direct from a wax model. The model is invested in Plaster-of-Paris or close packed sand. Molten metal is poured into the Plaster-of-Paris replacing the wax which melts away.

Claw-Set

The method of mounting gem stones in which the stone is held by tiny claws pressed over the crown facets.

Cloisonné

A process of enamelling, in which narrow strips of gold or silver are bent to form cells and soldered to a solid base. The cells are then filled with enamel.

Collet Set

A development of box setting in which the sides of the box are filled down to expose more of the gemstone to the light. As a result, the setting edge is reduced to four claws.

Damascene

The method of incrusting metals with other, usually more precious metals, once practised mainly in Damascus.

Embossing

The process of raising a domed design on the front of the metal by beating it with punches and a hammer from behind.

Engraving

A linear pattern achieved by cutting away the surface of the metal with a sharp pointed tool called a graver.

Filigree

Ornamental work of fine gold or silver wire formed into delicate tracery.

Foil

A thin leaf of metal placed behind a gem stone or a paste in order to heighten its colour or brilliance.

Gipsy Setting

A setting in which the surface of the gemstone is scarcely above the level of the surrounding metal. The setting edge is continuous, raised with a scoper from the surrounding metal. Frequently employed for signet rings.

Granulated Work

Work in which minute bead or grains of gold form a raised surface decoration. The grains are not soldered but fused with the gold surface through the use of copper carbonate.

Grisaille

Painting in grey monochrome, sometimes used in metalwork.

Intaglio

A carved design hollowed out of the surface of a gem (in contrast to cameo, in which the background is cut away).

Millegrain

A setting in which tiny beads or grains grip the girdle or widest part of the stone.

Niello

A black alloy of sulphur, lead, silver and copper used in decorating engraved work on silver or gold.

Opus Interassile

The method of piercing an open pattern in metal with a chisel not a saw, introduced by the Romans.

Pavé Setting

The method of setting stones very close together so that very little metal shows between them.

Piercing

The method of cutting with a saw an open design in a piece of metal.

Piqué

The process of inlaying tortoiseshell with tiny beads or lines of gold.

Plique-à-jour

A method of enamelling in which the backing is removed so that the effect is of a stained glass window.

Repoussé

Decorative process of raising a domed pattern on the front of gold or silver by beating it with a hammer and punches from behind.

ABOVE The stages of conversion of a perfect octahedral diamond crystal into a brilliant cut stone.

BELOW The brilliant cut with 58 facets and the rose cut with 24 facets.

Outline of cuts

A Baton

B obus

C calibre

D trapeze

E lozenge

F navette

G lunette

H marquise or navette

I cut cornered triangle

J triangle

K kite

L keystone

Conventional styles of gem cutting

Models of doublets or composite stones

ABCD	cabochon cuts	J	pendeloque
EF	trap or step cut showing base and top plan	K	cushion cut
		L	oblong step or trap cut
G	square cut	MN	scissors or cross cut
H	marquise	OP	faceted beads
I	fancy star	Q	Briolette

g organizations
ice the pictures

p right   Institute of Geological Sciences   63 top right, 81 top left, 86,
                           87, left, 87 right, 88, 89, 90, 91, 92, 93
                           William Macquity   12 bottom, 14 bottom, 17 bottom
                           S J Phillip Ltd.   29, 30 top, 32 centre, 32 top, 33, 34, 35, 44,
                               49, 57 top, 74 top right
tom   Alison Richards   77 top left
                           Joseph Sataloff   8, 13, 26, 27 top, 28 bottom, 32 bottom,
                               39 cent 39 top left, 42, 43, 48, 51, 52 top, 52 bottom 53,
, 60 top left   54, 55, 56, 57 bottom, 58, 62, 64, 65 top left 66, 68, 69,
tom   70, 71, 72, 82, 83 bottom
                           Scala, Milan   20, 21, 22 bottom, 24, 25, 50
                           Charles De Temple 75 bottom right
                           Wartski Ltd   67
1, 14 top and   Ziolo   2–3, 16 bottom, 22 top, 81 top left, 83 top 36, 37
ottom 31, 37   top left
60 top right,   Jewelry for the jacket   loaned by N Bloom & Son Ltd and
                           photographed by Melvin Grey